My Health

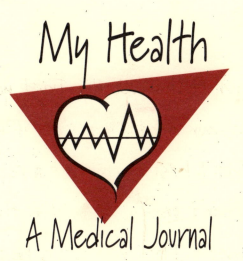

A Medical Journal

The "*Write It Down!*"® Series
by Journals Unlimited, Inc.

Printed in the USA using recycled materials.

You are your own best advocate. Trust your instincts, always ask your doctor questions if you don't understand. Don't hesitate to get a second opinion. If you still don't understand, have the doctor "Write-It-Down!"® The internet is helpful in doing your own research. It is a good idea to request copies of all diagnostic tests, including routine blood work. This is useful to compare results from year to year and recognize any changes in your health.

Health Statistics

Name: _____

Birth date: _____ Height: _____ Blood type: _____

	Current	Goal	As of	As of	As of	As of
Date:	_____	_____	_____	_____	_____	_____
Weight:	_____	_____	_____	_____	_____	_____
BMI:	_____	_____	_____	_____	_____	_____
Blood Pressure:	_____	_____	_____	_____	_____	_____
Cholesterol:	_____	_____	_____	_____	_____	_____
Blood Glucose:	_____	_____	_____	_____	_____	_____

Immunizations

Type	Date	Type	Date	Type	Date
_____	_____	_____	_____	_____	_____
_____	_____	_____	_____	_____	_____
_____	_____	_____	_____	_____	_____
_____	_____	_____	_____	_____	_____

Test

Test	Date	Date	Date	Date	Date	Date
Mammogram	_____	_____	_____	_____	_____	_____
Pap test	_____	_____	_____	_____	_____	_____
Prostate exam	_____	_____	_____	_____	_____	_____
Blood work	_____	_____	_____	_____	_____	_____
Urinalysis	_____	_____	_____	_____	_____	_____
Colonoscopy	_____	_____	_____	_____	_____	_____
Fasting blood sugar	_____	_____	_____	_____	_____	_____
Bone density	_____	_____	_____	_____	_____	_____
Hearing	_____	_____	_____	_____	_____	_____
Vision	_____	_____	_____	_____	_____	_____
Dental	_____	_____	_____	_____	_____	_____
Tetanus shot	_____	_____	_____	_____	_____	_____
Flu shot (seasonal)	_____	_____	_____	_____	_____	_____
_____	_____	_____	_____	_____	_____	_____
_____	_____	_____	_____	_____	_____	_____
_____	_____	_____	_____	_____	_____	_____
_____	_____	_____	_____	_____	_____	_____
_____	_____	_____	_____	_____	_____	_____

Surgeries

Surgery type:	Reason:	Doctor:	Date:
_____	_____	_____	_____
_____	_____	_____	_____
_____	_____	_____	_____
_____	_____	_____	_____
_____	_____	_____	_____

Family Health History

	Mother	Grandparents (M)	Father	Grandparents (F)
Heart Disease				
Diabetes				
Cancer				
Liver Disease				
Stroke				
Thyroid (H/L)				
Depression/Suicide				
Epilepsy				
Kidney Disease				

Physicians

Name	Speciality	Address	Phone

Medications

Name	Dosage	Prescribed by	Prescribed for	Start-End Date

Date: _____

Doctor's name: _____

Facility name / Phone: _____

Reason for visit: _____

_____

Symptoms: _____

_____

_____

_____

Questions: _____

_____

_____

Doctor's advice/Procedure performed: _____

_____

_____

_____

_____

_____

Plan of action: _____

_____

_____

Prescribed medications: _____

_____

Follow up required: _____

_____

_____

_____

_____

_____

Weight: _____ Blood Pressure: _____ Heart Rate: _____ Temp: _____

Prescribed Diagnostic Tests

Date: _____ Test ordered by: _____

Name of laboratory / hospital / facility: _____

Name of attending physician / laboratory rep: _____

Name of diagnostic test: _____

_____

Reason for test: _____

_____

Prep for test: _____

_____

Results of test: _____

_____

_____

_____

Date: _____ Test ordered by: _____

Name of laboratory / hospital / facility: _____

Name of attending physician / laboratory rep: _____

Name of diagnostic test: _____

_____

Reason for test: _____

_____

Prep for test: _____

_____

Results of test: _____

_____

_____

_____

Date: _____

Doctor's name: _____

Facility name / Phone: _____

Reason for visit: _____

Symptoms: _____

_____

_____

Questions: _____

_____

Doctor's advice/Procedure performed: _____

_____

_____

_____

_____

Plan of action: _____

_____

_____

Prescribed medications: _____

_____

Follow up required: _____

_____

_____

_____

_____

_____

Weight: _____ Blood Pressure: _____ Heart Rate: _____ Temp: _____

Prescribed Diagnostic Tests

Date: _____ Test ordered by:_____

Name of laboratory / hospital / facility: _____

Name of attending physician / laboratory rep:_____

Name of diagnostic test:_____

_____

Reason for test:_____

_____

Prep for test: _____

_____

Results of test: _____

_____

_____

_____

Date: _____ Test ordered by:_____

Name of laboratory / hospital / facility: _____

Name of attending physician / laboratory rep:_____

Name of diagnostic test:_____

_____

Reason for test:_____

_____

Prep for test: _____

_____

Results of test: _____

_____

_____

_____

Date: _____

Doctor's name: _____

Facility name / Phone: _____

Reason for visit: _____

_____

Symptoms: _____

_____

_____

_____

Questions: _____

_____

_____

Doctor's advice/Procedure performed: _____

_____

_____

_____

_____

Plan of action: _____

_____

_____

Prescribed medications: _____

_____

Follow up required: _____

_____

_____

_____

_____

Weight: _____ Blood Pressure: _____ Heart Rate: _____ Temp: _____

Prescribed Diagnostic Tests

Date: _____ Test ordered by: _____

Name of laboratory / hospital / facility: _____

Name of attending physician / laboratory rep: _____

Name of diagnostic test: _____

_____

Reason for test: _____

_____

Prep for test: _____

_____

Results of test: _____

_____

_____

_____

Date: _____ Test ordered by: _____

Name of laboratory / hospital / facility: _____

Name of attending physician / laboratory rep: _____

Name of diagnostic test: _____

_____

Reason for test: _____

_____

Prep for test: _____

_____

Results of test: _____

_____

_____

_____

Date: _____

Doctor's name: _____

Facility name / Phone: _____

Reason for visit: _____

_____

Symptoms: _____

_____

_____

_____

Questions: _____

_____

_____

_____

Doctor's advice/Procedure performed: _____

_____

_____

_____

_____

_____

Plan of action: _____

_____

_____

_____

Prescribed medications: _____

_____

Follow up required: _____

_____

_____

_____

_____

_____

Weight: _____ Blood Pressure: _____ Heart Rate: _____ Temp: _____

Prescribed Diagnostic Tests

Date: _____ Test ordered by: _____

Name of laboratory / hospital / facility: _____

Name of attending physician / laboratory rep: _____

Name of diagnostic test: _____

_____

Reason for test: _____

_____

Prep for test: _____

_____

Results of test: _____

_____

_____

_____

_____

Date: _____ Test ordered by: _____

Name of laboratory / hospital / facility: _____

Name of attending physician / laboratory rep: _____

Name of diagnostic test: _____

_____

Reason for test: _____

_____

Prep for test: _____

_____

Results of test: _____

_____

_____

_____

Date: _____

Doctor's name: _____

Facility name / Phone: _____

Reason for visit: _____

Symptoms: _____

_____

_____

_____

Questions: _____

_____

_____

Doctor's advice/Procedure performed: _____

_____

_____

_____

_____

Plan of action: _____

_____

_____

Prescribed medications: _____

_____

Follow up required: _____

_____

_____

_____

_____

Weight: _____ Blood Pressure: _____ Heart Rate: _____ Temp: _____

Prescribed Diagnostic Tests

Date: _____ Test ordered by:_____

Name of laboratory / hospital / facility: _____

Name of attending physician / laboratory rep:_____

Name of diagnostic test: _____

_____

Reason for test:_____

_____

Prep for test: _____

_____

Results of test: _____

_____

_____

_____

Date: _____ Test ordered by:_____

Name of laboratory / hospital / facility: _____

Name of attending physician / laboratory rep:_____

Name of diagnostic test: _____

_____

Reason for test:_____

_____

Prep for test: _____

_____

Results of test: _____

_____

_____

_____

Date: _____

Doctor's name: _____

Facility name / Phone: _____

Reason for visit: _____

_____

Symptoms: _____

_____

_____

_____

Questions: _____

_____

_____

Doctor's advice/Procedure performed: _____

_____

_____

_____

_____

Plan of action: _____

_____

_____

Prescribed medications: _____

_____

Follow up required: _____

_____

_____

_____

_____

_____

Weight: _____ Blood Pressure: _____ Heart Rate: _____ Temp: _____

Prescribed Diagnostic Tests

Date: _____ Test ordered by: _____

Name of laboratory / hospital / facility: _____

Name of attending physician / laboratory rep: _____

Name of diagnostic test: _____

_____

Reason for test: _____

_____

Prep for test: _____

_____

Results of test: _____

_____

_____

_____

_____

Date: _____ Test ordered by: _____

Name of laboratory / hospital / facility: _____

Name of attending physician / laboratory rep: _____

Name of diagnostic test: _____

_____

Reason for test: _____

_____

Prep for test: _____

_____

Results of test: _____

_____

_____

_____

Date: _____

Doctor's name: _____

Facility name / Phone: _____

Reason for visit: _____

Symptoms: _____

_____

_____

Questions: _____

_____

_____

Doctor's advice/Procedure performed: _____

_____

_____

_____

_____

Plan of action: _____

_____

_____

Prescribed medications: _____

_____

Follow up required: _____

_____

_____

_____

_____

Weight: _____ Blood Pressure: _____ Heart Rate: _____ Temp: _____

Prescribed Diagnostic Tests

Date: _____ Test ordered by: _____

Name of laboratory / hospital / facility: _____

Name of attending physician / laboratory rep: _____

Name of diagnostic test: _____

_____

Reason for test: _____

_____

Prep for test: _____

_____

Results of test: _____

_____

_____

_____

Date: _____ Test ordered by: _____

Name of laboratory / hospital / facility: _____

Name of attending physician / laboratory rep: _____

Name of diagnostic test: _____

_____

Reason for test: _____

_____

Prep for test: _____

_____

Results of test: _____

_____

_____

_____

Date: _____

Doctor's name: _____

Facility name / Phone: _____

Reason for visit: _____

_____

Symptoms: _____

_____

_____

_____

Questions: _____

_____

_____

Doctor's advice/Procedure performed: _____

_____

_____

_____

_____

_____

Plan of action: _____

_____

_____

Prescribed medications: _____

_____

Follow up required: _____

_____

_____

_____

_____

_____

Weight: _____ Blood Pressure: _____ Heart Rate: _____ Temp: _____

Prescribed Diagnostic Tests

Date: _____ Test ordered by: _____

Name of laboratory / hospital / facility: _____

Name of attending physician / laboratory rep: _____

Name of diagnostic test: _____

_____

Reason for test: _____

_____

Prep for test: _____

_____

Results of test: _____

_____

_____

_____

_____

Date: _____ Test ordered by: _____

Name of laboratory / hospital / facility: _____

Name of attending physician / laboratory rep: _____

Name of diagnostic test: _____

_____

Reason for test: _____

_____

Prep for test: _____

_____

Results of test: _____

_____

_____

_____

Date: _____

Doctor's name: _____

Facility name / Phone: _____

Reason for visit: _____

_____

Symptoms: _____

_____

_____

_____

Questions: _____

_____

_____

_____

Doctor's advice/Procedure performed: _____

_____

_____

_____

_____

_____

Plan of action: _____

_____

_____

Prescribed medications: _____

_____

Follow up required: _____

_____

_____

_____

_____

_____

Weight: _____ Blood Pressure: _____ Heart Rate: _____ Temp: _____

Prescribed Diagnostic Tests

Date: _____ Test ordered by: _____

Name of laboratory / hospital / facility: _____

Name of attending physician / laboratory rep: _____

Name of diagnostic test: _____

_____

Reason for test: _____

_____

Prep for test: _____

_____

Results of test: _____

_____

_____

_____

_____

Date: _____ Test ordered by: _____

Name of laboratory / hospital / facility: _____

Name of attending physician / laboratory rep: _____

Name of diagnostic test: _____

_____

Reason for test: _____

_____

Prep for test: _____

_____

Results of test: _____

_____

_____

_____

Date: _____

Doctor's name: _____

Facility name / Phone: _____

Reason for visit: _____

Symptoms: _____

_____

_____

_____

Questions: _____

_____

_____

_____

Doctor's advice/Procedure performed: _____

_____

_____

_____

_____

_____

Plan of action: _____

_____

_____

Prescribed medications: _____

_____

Follow up required: _____

_____

_____

_____

_____

_____

Weight: _____ Blood Pressure: _____ Heart Rate: _____ Temp: _____

Prescribed Diagnostic Tests

Date: _____ Test ordered by:_____

Name of laboratory / hospital / facility: _____

Name of attending physician / laboratory rep:_____

Name of diagnostic test:_____

_____

Reason for test:_____

_____

Prep for test: _____

_____

Results of test: _____

_____

_____

_____

Date: _____ Test ordered by:_____

Name of laboratory / hospital / facility: _____

Name of attending physician / laboratory rep:_____

Name of diagnostic test:_____

_____

Reason for test:_____

_____

Prep for test: _____

_____

Results of test: _____

_____

_____

_____

Date: _____

Doctor's name: _____

Facility name / Phone: _____

Reason for visit: _____

_____

Symptoms: _____

_____

_____

_____

Questions: _____

_____

_____

Doctor's advice/Procedure performed: _____

_____

_____

_____

_____

Plan of action: _____

_____

_____

Prescribed medications: _____

_____

Follow up required: _____

_____

_____

_____

_____

Weight: _____ Blood Pressure: _____ Heart Rate: _____ Temp: _____

Prescribed Diagnostic Tests

Date: _____ Test ordered by:_____

Name of laboratory / hospital / facility: _____

Name of attending physician / laboratory rep:_____

Name of diagnostic test: _____

_____

Reason for test:_____

_____

Prep for test: _____

_____

Results of test: _____

_____

_____

_____

_____

Date: _____ Test ordered by:_____

Name of laboratory / hospital / facility: _____

Name of attending physician / laboratory rep:_____

Name of diagnostic test: _____

_____

Reason for test:_____

_____

Prep for test: _____

_____

Results of test: _____

_____

_____

_____

Date: _____

Doctor's name: _____

Facility name / Phone: _____

Reason for visit: _____

Symptoms: _____

_____

_____

_____

Questions: _____

_____

_____

Doctor's advice/Procedure performed: _____

_____

_____

_____

_____

Plan of action: _____

_____

_____

Prescribed medications: _____

_____

Follow up required: _____

_____

_____

_____

_____

_____

Weight: _____ Blood Pressure: _____ Heart Rate: _____ Temp: _____

Prescribed Diagnostic Tests

Date: _____ Test ordered by:_____

Name of laboratory / hospital / facility: _____

Name of attending physician / laboratory rep:_____

Name of diagnostic test: _____

_____

Reason for test:_____

_____

Prep for test: _____

_____

Results of test: _____

_____

_____

_____

_____

Date: _____ Test ordered by:_____

Name of laboratory / hospital / facility: _____

Name of attending physician / laboratory rep:_____

Name of diagnostic test:_____

_____

Reason for test:_____

_____

Prep for test: _____

_____

Results of test: _____

_____

_____

_____

Date: _____

Doctor's name: _____

Facility name / Phone: _____

Reason for visit: _____

Symptoms: _____

_____

_____

_____

Questions: _____

_____

_____

Doctor's advice/Procedure performed: _____

_____

_____

_____

_____

Plan of action: _____

_____

_____

Prescribed medications: _____

_____

Follow up required: _____

_____

_____

_____

_____

Weight: _____ Blood Pressure: _____ Heart Rate: _____ Temp: _____

Prescribed Diagnostic Tests

Date: _____ Test ordered by:_____

Name of laboratory / hospital / facility: _____

Name of attending physician / laboratory rep:_____

Name of diagnostic test: _____

_____

Reason for test:_____

_____

Prep for test: _____

_____

Results of test: _____

_____

_____

_____

Date: _____ Test ordered by:_____

Name of laboratory / hospital / facility: _____

Name of attending physician / laboratory rep:_____

Name of diagnostic test: _____

_____

Reason for test:_____

_____

Prep for test: _____

_____

Results of test: _____

_____

_____

_____

Date: _____

Doctor's name: _____

Facility name / Phone: _____

Reason for visit: _____

_____

Symptoms: _____

_____

_____

_____

Questions: _____

_____

_____

Doctor's advice/Procedure performed: _____

_____

_____

_____

_____

Plan of action: _____

_____

_____

Prescribed medications: _____

_____

Follow up required: _____

_____

_____

_____

_____

_____

Weight: _____ Blood Pressure: _____ Heart Rate: _____ Temp: _____

Prescribed Diagnostic Tests

Date: _____ Test ordered by: _____

Name of laboratory / hospital / facility: _____

Name of attending physician / laboratory rep: _____

Name of diagnostic test: _____

_____

Reason for test: _____

_____

Prep for test: _____

_____

Results of test: _____

_____

_____

_____

_____

Date: _____ Test ordered by: _____

Name of laboratory / hospital / facility: _____

Name of attending physician / laboratory rep: _____

Name of diagnostic test: _____

_____

Reason for test: _____

_____

Prep for test: _____

_____

Results of test: _____

_____

_____

_____

Date: _____

Doctor's name: _____

Facility name / Phone: _____

Reason for visit: _____

_____

Symptoms: _____

_____

_____

_____

Questions: _____

_____

_____

Doctor's advice/Procedure performed: _____

_____

_____

_____

_____

Plan of action: _____

_____

_____

Prescribed medications: _____

_____

Follow up required: _____

_____

_____

_____

_____

Weight: _____ Blood Pressure: _____ Heart Rate: _____ Temp: _____

Prescribed Diagnostic Tests

Date: _____ Test ordered by: _____

Name of laboratory / hospital / facility: _____

Name of attending physician / laboratory rep: _____

Name of diagnostic test: _____

_____

Reason for test: _____

_____

Prep for test: _____

_____

Results of test: _____

_____

_____

_____

Date: _____ Test ordered by: _____

Name of laboratory / hospital / facility: _____

Name of attending physician / laboratory rep: _____

Name of diagnostic test: _____

_____

Reason for test: _____

_____

Prep for test: _____

_____

Results of test: _____

_____

_____

_____

Date: _____

Doctor's name: _____

Facility name / Phone: _____

Reason for visit: _____

_____

Symptoms: _____

_____

_____

_____

Questions: _____

_____

_____

_____

Doctor's advice/Procedure performed: ____

_____

_____

_____

_____

_____

Plan of action: _____

_____

_____

Prescribed medications: _____

_____

Follow up required: _____

_____

_____

_____

_____

_____

Weight: _____ Blood Pressure: _____ Heart Rate: _____ Temp: _____

Prescribed Diagnostic Tests

Date: _____ Test ordered by: _____

Name of laboratory / hospital / facility: _____

Name of attending physician / laboratory rep: _____

Name of diagnostic test: _____

_____

Reason for test: _____

_____

Prep for test: _____

_____

Results of test: _____

_____

_____

_____

_____

Date: _____ Test ordered by: _____

Name of laboratory / hospital / facility: _____

Name of attending physician / laboratory rep: _____

Name of diagnostic test: _____

_____

Reason for test: _____

_____

Prep for test: _____

_____

Results of test: _____

_____

_____

_____

Date: _____

Doctor's name: _____

Facility name / Phone: _____

Reason for visit: _____

_____

Symptoms: _____

_____

_____

_____

Questions: _____

_____

_____

Doctor's advice/Procedure performed: _____

_____

_____

_____

_____

Plan of action: _____

_____

_____

Prescribed medications: _____

_____

Follow up required: _____

_____

_____

_____

_____

_____

Weight: _____ Blood Pressure: _____ Heart Rate: _____ Temp: _____

Prescribed Diagnostic Tests

Date: _____ Test ordered by: _____

Name of laboratory / hospital / facility: _____

Name of attending physician / laboratory rep: _____

Name of diagnostic test: _____

_____

Reason for test: _____

_____

Prep for test: _____

_____

Results of test: _____

_____

_____

_____

_____

Date: _____ Test ordered by: _____

Name of laboratory / hospital / facility: _____

Name of attending physician / laboratory rep: _____

Name of diagnostic test: _____

_____

Reason for test: _____

_____

Prep for test: _____

_____

Results of test: _____

_____

_____

_____

_____

Date: _____

Doctor's name: _____

Facility name / Phone: _____

Reason for visit: _____

Symptoms: _____
_____
_____
_____

Questions: _____
_____
_____

Doctor's advice/Procedure performed: _____
_____
_____
_____

Plan of action: _____
_____
_____

Prescribed medications: _____

Follow up required: _____
_____
_____
_____
_____

Weight: _____ Blood Pressure: _____ Heart Rate: _____ Temp: _____

Prescribed Diagnostic Tests

Date: _____ Test ordered by: _____

Name of laboratory / hospital / facility: _____

Name of attending physician / laboratory rep: _____

Name of diagnostic test: _____

_____

Reason for test: _____

_____

Prep for test: _____

_____

Results of test: _____

_____

_____

_____

_____

Date: _____ Test ordered by: _____

Name of laboratory / hospital / facility: _____

Name of attending physician / laboratory rep: _____

Name of diagnostic test: _____

_____

Reason for test: _____

_____

Prep for test: _____

_____

Results of test: _____

_____

_____

_____

Date: _____

Doctor's name: _____

Facility name / Phone: _____

Reason for visit: _____

Symptoms: _____

_____

_____

_____

Questions: _____

_____

_____

Doctor's advice/Procedure performed: _____

_____

_____

_____

_____

_____

Plan of action: _____

_____

_____

Prescribed medications: _____

_____

Follow up required: _____

_____

_____

_____

_____

_____

Weight: _____ Blood Pressure: _____ Heart Rate: _____ Temp: _____

Prescribed Diagnostic Tests

Date: _____ Test ordered by: _____

Name of laboratory / hospital / facility: _____

Name of attending physician / laboratory rep: _____

Name of diagnostic test: _____

_____

Reason for test: _____

_____

Prep for test: _____

_____

Results of test: _____

_____

_____

_____

Date: _____ Test ordered by: _____

Name of laboratory / hospital / facility: _____

Name of attending physician / laboratory rep: _____

Name of diagnostic test: _____

_____

Reason for test: _____

_____

Prep for test: _____

_____

Results of test: _____

_____

_____

_____

Date: _____

Doctor's name: _____

Facility name / Phone: _____

Reason for visit: _____

Symptoms: _____

_____

_____

_____

Questions: _____

_____

_____

Doctor's advice/Procedure performed: _____

_____

_____

_____

_____

Plan of action: _____

_____

_____

Prescribed medications: _____

_____

Follow up required: _____

_____

_____

_____

_____

Weight: _____ Blood Pressure: _____ Heart Rate: _____ Temp: _____

Prescribed Diagnostic Tests

Date: _____ Test ordered by: _____

Name of laboratory / hospital / facility: _____

Name of attending physician / laboratory rep: _____

Name of diagnostic test: _____

_____

Reason for test: _____

_____

Prep for test: _____

Results of test: _____

_____

_____

_____

Date: _____ Test ordered by: _____

Name of laboratory / hospital / facility: _____

Name of attending physician / laboratory rep: _____

Name of diagnostic test: _____

_____

Reason for test: _____

_____

Prep for test: _____

Results of test: _____

_____

_____

_____

Date: _____

Doctor's name: _____

Facility name / Phone: _____

Reason for visit: _____

_____

Symptoms: _____

_____

_____

_____

Questions: _____

_____

_____

Doctor's advice/Procedure performed: _____

_____

_____

_____

_____

_____

Plan of action: _____

_____

_____

Prescribed medications: _____

_____

Follow up required: _____

_____

_____

_____

_____

_____

Weight: _____ Blood Pressure: _____ Heart Rate: _____ Temp: _____

Prescribed Diagnostic Tests

Date: _____ Test ordered by: _____

Name of laboratory / hospital / facility: _____

Name of attending physician / laboratory rep: _____

Name of diagnostic test: _____

_____

Reason for test: _____

_____

Prep for test: _____

_____

Results of test: _____

_____

_____

_____

_____

Date: _____ Test ordered by: _____

Name of laboratory / hospital / facility: _____

Name of attending physician / laboratory rep: _____

Name of diagnostic test: _____

_____

Reason for test: _____

_____

Prep for test: _____

_____

Results of test: _____

_____

_____

_____

Date: _____

Doctor's name: _____

Facility name / Phone: _____

Reason for visit: _____

_____

Symptoms: _____

_____

_____

_____

Questions: _____

_____

_____

Doctor's advice/Procedure performed: _____

_____

_____

_____

_____

_____

Plan of action: _____

_____

_____

Prescribed medications: _____

_____

Follow up required: _____

_____

_____

_____

_____

_____

Weight: _____ Blood Pressure: _____ Heart Rate: _____ Temp: _____

Prescribed Diagnostic Tests

Date: _____ Test ordered by: _____

Name of laboratory / hospital / facility: _____

Name of attending physician / laboratory rep: _____

Name of diagnostic test: _____

_____

Reason for test: _____

_____

Prep for test: _____

_____

Results of test: _____

_____

_____

_____

Date: _____ Test ordered by: _____

Name of laboratory / hospital / facility: _____

Name of attending physician / laboratory rep: _____

Name of diagnostic test: _____

_____

Reason for test: _____

_____

Prep for test: _____

_____

Results of test: _____

_____

_____

_____

Date: _____

Doctor's name: _____

Facility name / Phone: _____

Reason for visit: _____

Symptoms: _____

_____

_____

_____

Questions: _____

_____

_____

Doctor's advice/Procedure performed: _____

_____

_____

_____

_____

_____

Plan of action: _____

_____

_____

Prescribed medications: _____

_____

Follow up required: _____

_____

_____

_____

_____

_____

Weight: _____ Blood Pressure: _____ Heart Rate: _____ Temp: _____

Prescribed Diagnostic Tests

Date: _____ Test ordered by:_____

Name of laboratory / hospital / facility: _____

Name of attending physician / laboratory rep:_____

Name of diagnostic test: _____

_____

Reason for test:_____

_____

Prep for test: _____

_____

Results of test: _____

_____

_____

_____

Date: _____ Test ordered by:_____

Name of laboratory / hospital / facility: _____

Name of attending physician / laboratory rep:_____

Name of diagnostic test: _____

_____

Reason for test:_____

_____

Prep for test: _____

_____

Results of test: _____

_____

_____

_____

Date: _____

Doctor's name: _____

Facility name / Phone: _____

Reason for visit: _____
_____

Symptoms: _____
_____
_____
_____

Questions: _____
_____
_____

Doctor's advice/Procedure performed: _____
_____
_____
_____
_____

Plan of action: _____
_____
_____

Prescribed medications: _____
_____

Follow up required: _____
_____
_____
_____
_____

Weight: _____ Blood Pressure: _____ Heart Rate: _____ Temp: _____

Prescribed Diagnostic Tests

Date: _____ Test ordered by:_____

Name of laboratory / hospital / facility: _____

Name of attending physician / laboratory rep: _____

Name of diagnostic test: _____

_____

Reason for test:_____

_____

Prep for test: _____

_____

Results of test: _____

_____

_____

_____

Date: _____ Test ordered by:_____

Name of laboratory / hospital / facility: _____

Name of attending physician / laboratory rep: _____

Name of diagnostic test: _____

_____

Reason for test:_____

_____

Prep for test: _____

_____

Results of test: _____

_____

_____

_____

Date: _____

Doctor's name: _____

Facility name / Phone: _____

Reason for visit: _____

Symptoms: _____
_____
_____
_____

Questions: _____
_____
_____

Doctor's advice/Procedure performed: _____
_____
_____
_____
_____

Plan of action: _____
_____
_____

Prescribed medications: _____
_____

Follow up required: _____
_____
_____
_____
_____

Weight: _____ Blood Pressure: _____ Heart Rate: _____ Temp: _____

Prescribed Diagnostic Tests

Date: _____ Test ordered by: _____

Name of laboratory / hospital / facility: _____

Name of attending physician / laboratory rep: _____

Name of diagnostic test: _____

_____

Reason for test: _____

_____

Prep for test: _____

_____

Results of test: _____

_____

_____

_____

Date: _____ Test ordered by: _____

Name of laboratory / hospital / facility: _____

Name of attending physician / laboratory rep: _____

Name of diagnostic test: _____

_____

Reason for test: _____

_____

Prep for test: _____

_____

Results of test: _____

_____

_____

_____

Date: _____

Doctor's name: _____

Facility name / Phone: _____

Reason for visit: _____

Symptoms: _____
_____
_____
_____

Questions: _____
_____
_____
_____

Doctor's advice/Procedure performed: _____
_____
_____
_____
_____
_____

Plan of action: _____
_____
_____

Prescribed medications: _____
_____

Follow up required: _____
_____
_____
_____
_____
_____

Weight: _____ Blood Pressure: _____ Heart Rate: _____ Temp: _____

Prescribed Diagnostic Tests

Date: _____ Test ordered by: _____

Name of laboratory / hospital / facility: _____

Name of attending physician / laboratory rep: _____

Name of diagnostic test: _____

_____

Reason for test: _____

_____

Prep for test: _____

_____

Results of test: _____

_____

_____

_____

_____

Date: _____ Test ordered by: _____

Name of laboratory / hospital / facility: _____

Name of attending physician / laboratory rep: _____

Name of diagnostic test: _____

_____

Reason for test: _____

_____

Prep for test: _____

_____

Results of test: _____

_____

_____

_____

Date: _____

Doctor's name: _____

Facility name / Phone: _____

Reason for visit: _____

_____

Symptoms: _____

_____

_____

_____

Questions: _____

_____

_____

Doctor's advice/Procedure performed: _____

_____

_____

_____

_____

_____

Plan of action: _____

_____

_____

Prescribed medications: _____

_____

Follow up required: _____

_____

_____

_____

_____

_____

Weight: _____ Blood Pressure: _____ Heart Rate: _____ Temp: _____

Prescribed Diagnostic Tests

Date: _____ Test ordered by: _____

Name of laboratory / hospital / facility: _____

Name of attending physician / laboratory rep: _____

Name of diagnostic test: _____

_____

Reason for test: _____

_____

Prep for test: _____

_____

Results of test: _____

_____

_____

_____

Date: _____ Test ordered by: _____

Name of laboratory / hospital / facility: _____

Name of attending physician / laboratory rep: _____

Name of diagnostic test: _____

_____

Reason for test: _____

_____

Prep for test: _____

_____

Results of test: _____

_____

_____

_____

Date: _____

Doctor's name: _____

Facility name / Phone: _____

Reason for visit: _____
_____

Symptoms: _____
_____
_____
_____

Questions: _____
_____
_____

Doctor's advice/Procedure performed: _____
_____
_____
_____
_____
_____

Plan of action: _____
_____
_____

Prescribed medications: _____
_____

Follow up required: _____
_____
_____
_____
_____
_____

Weight: _____ Blood Pressure: _____ Heart Rate: _____ Temp: _____

Prescribed Diagnostic Tests

Date: _____ Test ordered by: _____

Name of laboratory / hospital / facility: _____

Name of attending physician / laboratory rep: _____

Name of diagnostic test: _____

_____

Reason for test: _____

_____

Prep for test: _____

_____

Results of test: _____

_____

_____

_____

Date: _____ Test ordered by: _____

Name of laboratory / hospital / facility: _____

Name of attending physician / laboratory rep: _____

Name of diagnostic test: _____

_____

Reason for test: _____

_____

Prep for test: _____

_____

Results of test: _____

_____

_____

_____

Date: _____

Doctor's name: _____

Facility name / Phone: _____

Reason for visit: _____

Symptoms: _____

_____

_____

_____

Questions: _____

_____

_____

Doctor's advice/Procedure performed: _____

_____

_____

_____

_____

Plan of action: _____

_____

_____

Prescribed medications: _____

_____

Follow up required: _____

_____

_____

_____

_____

_____

Weight: _____ Blood Pressure: _____ Heart Rate: _____ Temp: _____

Prescribed Diagnostic Tests

Date: _____ Test ordered by: _____

Name of laboratory / hospital / facility: _____

Name of attending physician / laboratory rep: _____

Name of diagnostic test: _____

_____

Reason for test: _____

_____

Prep for test: _____

_____

Results of test: _____

_____

_____

_____

_____

Date: _____ Test ordered by: _____

Name of laboratory / hospital / facility: _____

Name of attending physician / laboratory rep: _____

Name of diagnostic test: _____

_____

Reason for test: _____

_____

Prep for test: _____

_____

Results of test: _____

_____

_____

_____

Date: _____

Doctor's name: _____

Facility name / Phone: _____

Reason for visit: _____

_____

Symptoms: _____

_____

_____

_____

Questions: _____

_____

_____

_____

Doctor's advice/Procedure performed: _____

_____

_____

_____

_____

_____

Plan of action: _____

_____

_____

Prescribed medications: _____

_____

Follow up required: _____

_____

_____

_____

_____

_____

Weight: _____ Blood Pressure: _____ Heart Rate: _____ Temp: _____

Prescribed Diagnostic Tests

Date: _____ Test ordered by: _____

Name of laboratory / hospital / facility: _____

Name of attending physician / laboratory rep: _____

Name of diagnostic test: _____

_____

Reason for test: _____

_____

Prep for test: _____

_____

Results of test: _____

_____

_____

_____

_____

Date: _____ Test ordered by: _____

Name of laboratory / hospital / facility: _____

Name of attending physician / laboratory rep: _____

Name of diagnostic test: _____

_____

Reason for test: _____

_____

Prep for test: _____

_____

Results of test: _____

_____

_____

_____

_____

Date: _____

Doctor's name: _____

Facility name / Phone: _____

Reason for visit: _____
_____

Symptoms: _____
_____
_____
_____

Questions: _____
_____
_____

Doctor's advice/Procedure performed: _____
_____
_____
_____
_____
_____

Plan of action: _____
_____
_____

Prescribed medications: _____
_____

Follow up required: _____
_____
_____
_____
_____
_____

Weight: _____ Blood Pressure: _____ Heart Rate: _____ Temp: _____

Prescribed Diagnostic Tests

Date: _____ Test ordered by: _____

Name of laboratory / hospital / facility: _____

Name of attending physician / laboratory rep: _____

Name of diagnostic test: _____

_____

Reason for test: _____

_____

Prep for test: _____

_____

Results of test: _____

_____

_____

_____

Date: _____ Test ordered by: _____

Name of laboratory / hospital / facility: _____

Name of attending physician / laboratory rep: _____

Name of diagnostic test: _____

_____

Reason for test: _____

_____

Prep for test: _____

_____

Results of test: _____

_____

_____

_____

Date: _____

Doctor's name: _____

Facility name / Phone: _____

Reason for visit: _____
_____

Symptoms: _____
_____
_____
_____

Questions: _____
_____
_____

Doctor's advice/Procedure performed: _____
_____
_____
_____
_____

Plan of action: _____
_____
_____

Prescribed medications: _____
_____

Follow up required: _____
_____
_____
_____
_____

Weight: _____ Blood Pressure: _____ Heart Rate: _____ Temp: _____

Prescribed Diagnostic Tests

Date: _____ Test ordered by: _____

Name of laboratory / hospital / facility: _____

Name of attending physician / laboratory rep: _____

Name of diagnostic test: _____

_____

Reason for test: _____

_____

Prep for test: _____

_____

Results of test: _____

_____

_____

_____

Date: _____ Test ordered by: _____

Name of laboratory / hospital / facility: _____

Name of attending physician / laboratory rep: _____

Name of diagnostic test: _____

_____

Reason for test: _____

_____

Prep for test: _____

_____

Results of test: _____

_____

_____

_____

Date: _____

Doctor's name: _____

Facility name / Phone: _____

Reason for visit: _____

Symptoms: _____
_____
_____
_____

Questions: _____
_____
_____

Doctor's advice/Procedure performed: _____
_____
_____
_____
_____

Plan of action: _____
_____
_____

Prescribed medications: _____
_____

Follow up required: _____
_____
_____
_____
_____

Weight: _____ Blood Pressure: _____ Heart Rate: _____ Temp: _____

Prescribed Diagnostic Tests

Date: _____ Test ordered by: _____

Name of laboratory / hospital / facility: _____

Name of attending physician / laboratory rep: _____

Name of diagnostic test: _____

_____

Reason for test: _____

_____

Prep for test: _____

_____

Results of test: _____

_____

_____

_____

Date: _____ Test ordered by: _____

Name of laboratory / hospital / facility: _____

Name of attending physician / laboratory rep: _____

Name of diagnostic test: _____

_____

Reason for test: _____

_____

Prep for test: _____

_____

Results of test: _____

_____

_____

_____

Date: _____

Doctor's name: _____

Facility name / Phone: _____

Reason for visit: _____

_____

Symptoms: _____

_____

_____

_____

Questions: _____

_____

_____

_____

Doctor's advice/Procedure performed: _____

_____

_____

_____

_____

_____

Plan of action: _____

_____

_____

Prescribed medications: _____

_____

Follow up required: _____

_____

_____

_____

_____

_____

Weight: _____ Blood Pressure: _____ Heart Rate: _____ Temp: _____

Prescribed Diagnostic Tests

Date: _____ Test ordered by: _____

Name of laboratory / hospital / facility: _____

Name of attending physician / laboratory rep: _____

Name of diagnostic test: _____
_____

Reason for test: _____
_____

Prep for test: _____
_____

Results of test: _____
_____
_____
_____
_____

Date: _____ Test ordered by: _____

Name of laboratory / hospital / facility: _____

Name of attending physician / laboratory rep: _____

Name of diagnostic test: _____
_____

Reason for test: _____
_____

Prep for test: _____
_____

Results of test: _____
_____
_____
_____

Date: _____

Doctor's name: _____

Facility name / Phone: _____

Reason for visit: _____

Symptoms: _____
_____
_____
_____

Questions: _____
_____
_____

Doctor's advice/Procedure performed: _____
_____
_____
_____
_____
_____

Plan of action: _____
_____
_____

Prescribed medications: _____
_____

Follow up required: _____
_____
_____
_____
_____
_____

Weight: _____ Blood Pressure: _____ Heart Rate: _____ Temp: _____

Prescribed Diagnostic Tests

Date: _____ Test ordered by:_____

Name of laboratory / hospital / facility: _____

Name of attending physician / laboratory rep:_____

Name of diagnostic test: _____

_____

Reason for test:_____

_____

Prep for test: _____

_____

Results of test: _____

_____

_____

_____

Date: _____ Test ordered by:_____

Name of laboratory / hospital / facility: _____

Name of attending physician / laboratory rep:_____

Name of diagnostic test: _____

_____

Reason for test:_____

_____

Prep for test: _____

_____

Results of test: _____

_____

_____

_____

Date: _____

Doctor's name: _____

Facility name / Phone: _____

Reason for visit: _____

_____

Symptoms: _____

_____

_____

_____

Questions: _____

_____

_____

Doctor's advice/Procedure performed: _____

_____

_____

_____

_____

_____

Plan of action: _____

_____

_____

Prescribed medications: _____

_____

Follow up required: _____

_____

_____

_____

_____

_____

Weight: _____ Blood Pressure: _____ Heart Rate: _____ Temp: _____

Prescribed Diagnostic Tests

Date: _____ Test ordered by: _____

Name of laboratory / hospital / facility: _____

Name of attending physician / laboratory rep: _____

Name of diagnostic test: _____

_____

Reason for test: _____

_____

Prep for test: _____

_____

Results of test: _____

_____

_____

_____

Date: _____ Test ordered by: _____

Name of laboratory / hospital / facility: _____

Name of attending physician / laboratory rep: _____

Name of diagnostic test: _____

_____

Reason for test: _____

_____

Prep for test: _____

_____

Results of test: _____

_____

_____

_____

Date: _____

Doctor's name: _____

Facility name / Phone: _____

Reason for visit: _____

_____

Symptoms: _____

_____

_____

_____

Questions: _____

_____

_____

Doctor's advice/Procedure performed: _____

_____

_____

_____

_____

_____

Plan of action: _____

_____

_____

Prescribed medications: _____

_____

Follow up required: _____

_____

_____

_____

_____

_____

Weight: _____ Blood Pressure: _____ Heart Rate: _____ Temp: _____

Prescribed Diagnostic Tests

Date: _____ Test ordered by: _____

Name of laboratory / hospital / facility: _____

Name of attending physician / laboratory rep: _____

Name of diagnostic test: _____

_____

Reason for test: _____

_____

Prep for test: _____

_____

Results of test: _____

_____

_____

_____

Date: _____ Test ordered by: _____

Name of laboratory / hospital / facility: _____

Name of attending physician / laboratory rep: _____

Name of diagnostic test: _____

_____

Reason for test: _____

_____

Prep for test: _____

_____

Results of test: _____

_____

_____

_____

Date: _____

Doctor's name: _____

Facility name / Phone: _____

Reason for visit: _____
_____

Symptoms: _____
_____
_____
_____

Questions: _____
_____
_____

Doctor's advice/Procedure performed: _____
_____
_____
_____
_____
_____

Plan of action: _____
_____
_____

Prescribed medications: _____
_____

Follow up required: _____
_____
_____
_____
_____
_____

Weight: _____ Blood Pressure: _____ Heart Rate: _____ Temp: _____

Prescribed Diagnostic Tests

Date: _____ Test ordered by: _____

Name of laboratory / hospital / facility: _____

Name of attending physician / laboratory rep: _____

Name of diagnostic test: _____

_____

Reason for test: _____

_____

Prep for test: _____

_____

Results of test: _____

_____

_____

_____

Date: _____ Test ordered by: _____

Name of laboratory / hospital / facility: _____

Name of attending physician / laboratory rep: _____

Name of diagnostic test: _____

_____

Reason for test: _____

_____

Prep for test: _____

_____

Results of test: _____

_____

_____

_____

Date: _____

Doctor's name: _____

Facility name / Phone: _____

Reason for visit: _____

_____

Symptoms: _____

_____

_____

_____

Questions: _____

_____

_____

Doctor's advice/Procedure performed: _____

_____

_____

_____

_____

_____

Plan of action: _____

_____

_____

Prescribed medications: _____

_____

Follow up required: _____

_____

_____

_____

_____

_____

Weight: _____ Blood Pressure: _____ Heart Rate: _____ Temp: _____

Prescribed Diagnostic Tests

Date: _____ Test ordered by:_____

Name of laboratory / hospital / facility: _____

Name of attending physician / laboratory rep:_____

Name of diagnostic test: _____

_____

Reason for test:_____

_____

Prep for test: _____

_____

Results of test: _____

_____

_____

_____

Date: _____ Test ordered by:_____

Name of laboratory / hospital / facility: _____

Name of attending physician / laboratory rep:_____

Name of diagnostic test: _____

_____

Reason for test:_____

_____

Prep for test: _____

_____

Results of test: _____

_____

_____

_____

Date: _____

Doctor's name: _____

Facility name / Phone: _____

Reason for visit: _____

_____

Symptoms: _____

_____

_____

_____

Questions: _____

_____

_____

_____

Doctor's advice/Procedure performed: _____

_____

_____

_____

_____

_____

Plan of action: _____

_____

_____

Prescribed medications: _____

_____

Follow up required: _____

_____

_____

_____

_____

_____

Weight: _____ Blood Pressure: _____ Heart Rate: _____ Temp: _____

Prescribed Diagnostic Tests

Date: _____ Test ordered by: _____

Name of laboratory / hospital / facility: _____

Name of attending physician / laboratory rep: _____

Name of diagnostic test: _____

_____

Reason for test: _____

_____

Prep for test: _____

_____

Results of test: _____

_____

_____

_____

Date: _____ Test ordered by: _____

Name of laboratory / hospital / facility: _____

Name of attending physician / laboratory rep: _____

Name of diagnostic test: _____

_____

Reason for test: _____

_____

Prep for test: _____

_____

Results of test: _____

_____

_____

_____

Date: _____

Doctor's name: _____

Facility name / Phone: _____

Reason for visit: _____

Symptoms: _____
_____
_____
_____

Questions: _____
_____
_____

Doctor's advice/Procedure performed: _____
_____
_____
_____
_____
_____

Plan of action: _____
_____
_____

Prescribed medications: _____
_____

Follow up required: _____
_____
_____
_____
_____
_____

Weight: _____ Blood Pressure: _____ Heart Rate: _____ Temp: _____

Prescribed Diagnostic Tests

Date: _____ Test ordered by: _____

Name of laboratory / hospital / facility: _____

Name of attending physician / laboratory rep: _____

Name of diagnostic test: _____

_____

Reason for test: _____

_____

Prep for test: _____

_____

Results of test: _____

_____

_____

_____

_____

Date: _____ Test ordered by: _____

Name of laboratory / hospital / facility: _____

Name of attending physician / laboratory rep: _____

Name of diagnostic test: _____

_____

Reason for test: _____

_____

Prep for test: _____

_____

Results of test: _____

_____

_____

_____

Date: _____

Doctor's name: _____

Facility name / Phone: _____

Reason for visit: _____

_____

Symptoms: _____

_____

_____

_____

Questions: _____

_____

_____

Doctor's advice/Procedure performed: _____

_____

_____

_____

_____

Plan of action: _____

_____

_____

Prescribed medications: _____

_____

Follow up required: _____

_____

_____

_____

_____

Weight: _____ Blood Pressure: _____ Heart Rate: _____ Temp: _____

Prescribed Diagnostic Tests

Date: _____ Test ordered by: _____

Name of laboratory / hospital / facility: _____

Name of attending physician / laboratory rep: _____

Name of diagnostic test: _____

_____

Reason for test: _____

_____

Prep for test: _____

_____

Results of test: _____

_____

_____

_____

Date: _____ Test ordered by: _____

Name of laboratory / hospital / facility: _____

Name of attending physician / laboratory rep: _____

Name of diagnostic test: _____

_____

Reason for test: _____

_____

Prep for test: _____

_____

Results of test: _____

_____

_____

_____

Date: _____

Doctor's name: _____

Facility name / Phone: _____

Reason for visit: _____

_____

Symptoms: _____

_____

_____

_____

Questions: _____

_____

_____

_____

Doctor's advice/Procedure performed: _____

_____

_____

_____

_____

_____

Plan of action: _____

_____

_____

Prescribed medications: _____

_____

Follow up required: _____

_____

_____

_____

_____

_____

Weight: _____ Blood Pressure: _____ Heart Rate: _____ Temp: _____

Prescribed Diagnostic Tests

Date: _____ Test ordered by: _____

Name of laboratory / hospital / facility: _____

Name of attending physician / laboratory rep: _____

Name of diagnostic test: _____

_____

Reason for test: _____

_____

Prep for test: _____

_____

Results of test: _____

_____

_____

_____

_____

Date: _____ Test ordered by: _____

Name of laboratory / hospital / facility: _____

Name of attending physician / laboratory rep: _____

Name of diagnostic test: _____

_____

Reason for test: _____

_____

Prep for test: _____

_____

Results of test: _____

_____

_____

_____

Date: _____

Doctor's name: _____

Facility name / Phone: _____

Reason for visit: _____

_____

Symptoms: _____

_____

_____

_____

Questions: _____

_____

_____

Doctor's advice/Procedure performed: _____

_____

_____

_____

_____

_____

Plan of action: _____

_____

_____

Prescribed medications: _____

_____

Follow up required: _____

_____

_____

_____

_____

_____

Weight: _____ Blood Pressure: _____ Heart Rate: _____ Temp: _____

Prescribed Diagnostic Tests

Date: _____ Test ordered by: _____

Name of laboratory / hospital / facility: _____

Name of attending physician / laboratory rep: _____

Name of diagnostic test: _____

_____

Reason for test: _____

_____

Prep for test: _____

_____

Results of test: _____

_____

_____

_____

_____

Date: _____ Test ordered by: _____

Name of laboratory / hospital / facility: _____

Name of attending physician / laboratory rep: _____

Name of diagnostic test: _____

_____

Reason for test: _____

_____

Prep for test: _____

_____

Results of test: _____

_____

_____

_____

Date: _____

Doctor's name: _____

Facility name / Phone: _____

Reason for visit: _____

_____

Symptoms: _____

_____

_____

_____

Questions: _____

_____

_____

Doctor's advice/Procedure performed: _____

_____

_____

_____

_____

Plan of action: _____

_____

_____

Prescribed medications: _____

_____

Follow up required: _____

_____

_____

_____

_____

Weight: _____ Blood Pressure: _____ Heart Rate: _____ Temp: _____

Prescribed Diagnostic Tests

Date: _____ Test ordered by: _____

Name of laboratory / hospital / facility: _____

Name of attending physician / laboratory rep: _____

Name of diagnostic test: _____

_____

Reason for test: _____

_____

Prep for test: _____

_____

Results of test: _____

_____

_____

_____

_____

Date: _____ Test ordered by: _____

Name of laboratory / hospital / facility: _____

Name of attending physician / laboratory rep: _____

Name of diagnostic test: _____

_____

Reason for test: _____

_____

Prep for test: _____

_____

Results of test: _____

_____

_____

_____

Date: _____

Doctor's name: _____

Facility name / Phone: _____

Reason for visit: _____

_____

Symptoms: _____

_____

_____

_____

Questions: _____

_____

_____

Doctor's advice/Procedure performed: _____

_____

_____

_____

_____

_____

Plan of action: _____

_____

_____

Prescribed medications: _____

_____

Follow up required: _____

_____

_____

_____

_____

_____

Weight: _____ Blood Pressure: _____ Heart Rate: _____ Temp: _____

Prescribed Diagnostic Tests

Date: _____ Test ordered by: _____

Name of laboratory / hospital / facility: _____

Name of attending physician / laboratory rep: _____

Name of diagnostic test: _____

_____

Reason for test: _____

_____

Prep for test: _____

_____

Results of test: _____

_____

_____

_____

_____

Date: _____ Test ordered by: _____

Name of laboratory / hospital / facility: _____

Name of attending physician / laboratory rep: _____

Name of diagnostic test: _____

_____

Reason for test: _____

_____

Prep for test: _____

_____

Results of test: _____

_____

_____

_____

Date: _____

Doctor's name: _____

Facility name / Phone: _____

Reason for visit: _____
_____

Symptoms: _____
_____
_____
_____

Questions: _____
_____
_____

Doctor's advice/Procedure performed: _____
_____
_____
_____
_____
_____

Plan of action: _____
_____
_____

Prescribed medications: _____
_____

Follow up required: _____
_____
_____
_____
_____

Weight: _____ Blood Pressure: _____ Heart Rate: _____ Temp: _____

Prescribed Diagnostic Tests

Date: _____ Test ordered by: _____

Name of laboratory / hospital / facility: _____

Name of attending physician / laboratory rep: _____

Name of diagnostic test: _____

_____

Reason for test: _____

_____

Prep for test: _____

_____

Results of test: _____

_____

_____

_____

Date: _____ Test ordered by: _____

Name of laboratory / hospital / facility: _____

Name of attending physician / laboratory rep: _____

Name of diagnostic test: _____

_____

Reason for test: _____

_____

Prep for test: _____

_____

Results of test: _____

_____

_____

_____

Date: _____

Doctor's name: _____

Facility name / Phone: _____

Reason for visit: _____

_____

Symptoms: _____

_____

_____

_____

Questions: _____

_____

_____

Doctor's advice/Procedure performed: _____

_____

_____

_____

_____

Plan of action: _____

_____

_____

Prescribed medications: _____

_____

Follow up required: _____

_____

_____

_____

_____

Weight: _____ Blood Pressure: _____ Heart Rate: _____ Temp: _____

Prescribed Diagnostic Tests

Date: _____ Test ordered by: _____

Name of laboratory / hospital / facility: _____

Name of attending physician / laboratory rep: _____

Name of diagnostic test: _____

_____

Reason for test: _____

_____

Prep for test: _____

_____

Results of test: _____

_____

_____

_____

Date: _____ Test ordered by: _____

Name of laboratory / hospital / facility: _____

Name of attending physician / laboratory rep: _____

Name of diagnostic test: _____

_____

Reason for test: _____

_____

Prep for test: _____

_____

Results of test: _____

_____

_____

_____

Date: _____

Doctor's name: _____

Facility name / Phone: _____

Reason for visit: _____

Symptoms: _____

_____

_____

_____

Questions: _____

_____

_____

Doctor's advice/Procedure performed: _____

_____

_____

_____

_____

Plan of action: _____

_____

_____

Prescribed medications: _____

_____

Follow up required: _____

_____

_____

_____

_____

_____

Weight: _____ Blood Pressure: _____ Heart Rate: _____ Temp: _____

Prescribed Diagnostic Tests

Date: _____ Test ordered by: _____

Name of laboratory / hospital / facility: _____

Name of attending physician / laboratory rep: _____

Name of diagnostic test: _____

_____

Reason for test: _____

_____

Prep for test: _____

_____

Results of test: _____

_____

_____

_____

_____

Date: _____ Test ordered by: _____

Name of laboratory / hospital / facility: _____

Name of attending physician / laboratory rep: _____

Name of diagnostic test: _____

_____

Reason for test: _____

_____

Prep for test: _____

_____

Results of test: _____

_____

_____

_____

Date: _____

Doctor's name: _____

Facility name / Phone: _____

Reason for visit: _____
_____

Symptoms: _____
_____
_____
_____

Questions: _____
_____
_____

Doctor's advice/Procedure performed: _____
_____
_____
_____
_____
_____

Plan of action: _____
_____
_____

Prescribed medications: _____
_____

Follow up required: _____
_____
_____
_____
_____
_____

Weight: _____ Blood Pressure: _____ Heart Rate: _____ Temp: _____

Prescribed Diagnostic Tests

Date: _____ Test ordered by: _____

Name of laboratory / hospital / facility: _____

Name of attending physician / laboratory rep: _____

Name of diagnostic test: _____

_____

Reason for test: _____

_____

Prep for test: _____

_____

Results of test: _____

_____

_____

_____

_____

Date: _____ Test ordered by: _____

Name of laboratory / hospital / facility: _____

Name of attending physician / laboratory rep: _____

Name of diagnostic test: _____

_____

Reason for test: _____

_____

Prep for test: _____

_____

Results of test: _____

_____

_____

_____

_____

Date: _____

Doctor's name: _____

Facility name / Phone: _____

Reason for visit: _____

Symptoms: _____

_____

_____

_____

Questions: _____

_____

_____

Doctor's advice/Procedure performed: _____

_____

_____

_____

_____

Plan of action: _____

_____

_____

Prescribed medications: _____

_____

Follow up required: _____

_____

_____

_____

_____

Weight: _____ Blood Pressure: _____ Heart Rate: _____ Temp: _____

Prescribed Diagnostic Tests

Date: _____ Test ordered by: _____

Name of laboratory / hospital / facility: _____

Name of attending physician / laboratory rep: _____

Name of diagnostic test: _____

_____

Reason for test: _____

_____

Prep for test: _____

_____

Results of test: _____

_____

_____

_____

Date: _____ Test ordered by: _____

Name of laboratory / hospital / facility: _____

Name of attending physician / laboratory rep: _____

Name of diagnostic test: _____

_____

Reason for test: _____

_____

Prep for test: _____

_____

Results of test: _____

_____

_____

_____

Date: _____

Doctor's name: _____

Facility name / Phone: _____

Reason for visit: _____

Symptoms: _____

_____

_____

_____

Questions: _____

_____

_____

Doctor's advice/Procedure performed: _____

_____

_____

_____

_____

Plan of action: _____

_____

_____

Prescribed medications: _____

_____

Follow up required: _____

_____

_____

_____

_____

_____

Weight: _____ Blood Pressure: _____ Heart Rate: _____ Temp: _____

Prescribed Diagnostic Tests

Date: _____ Test ordered by: _____

Name of laboratory / hospital / facility: _____

Name of attending physician / laboratory rep: _____

Name of diagnostic test: _____

_____

Reason for test: _____

_____

Prep for test: _____

_____

Results of test: _____

_____

_____

_____

_____

Date: _____ Test ordered by: _____

Name of laboratory / hospital / facility: _____

Name of attending physician / laboratory rep: _____

Name of diagnostic test: _____

_____

Reason for test: _____

_____

Prep for test: _____

_____

Results of test: _____

_____

_____

_____

Date: _____

Doctor's name: _____

Facility name / Phone: _____

Reason for visit: _____

Symptoms: _____

_____

_____

_____

Questions: _____

_____

_____

Doctor's advice/Procedure performed: _____

_____

_____

_____

_____

Plan of action: _____

_____

_____

Prescribed medications: _____

_____

Follow up required: _____

_____

_____

_____

_____

_____

Weight: _____ Blood Pressure: _____ Heart Rate: _____ Temp: _____

Prescribed Diagnostic Tests

Date: _____ Test ordered by:_____

Name of laboratory / hospital / facility: _____

Name of attending physician / laboratory rep:_____

Name of diagnostic test:_____

_____

Reason for test:_____

_____

Prep for test: _____

_____

Results of test: _____

_____

_____

_____

Date: _____ Test ordered by:_____

Name of laboratory / hospital / facility: _____

Name of attending physician / laboratory rep:_____

Name of diagnostic test:_____

_____

Reason for test:_____

_____

Prep for test: _____

_____

Results of test: _____

_____

_____

_____

Date: _____

Doctor's name: _____

Facility name / Phone: _____

Reason for visit: _____

_____

Symptoms: _____

_____

_____

_____

Questions: _____

_____

_____

Doctor's advice/Procedure performed: _____

_____

_____

_____

_____

Plan of action: _____

_____

_____

Prescribed medications: _____

_____

Follow up required: _____

_____

_____

_____

_____

_____

Weight: _____ Blood Pressure: _____ Heart Rate: _____ Temp: _____

Prescribed Diagnostic Tests

Date: _____ Test ordered by: _____

Name of laboratory / hospital / facility: _____

Name of attending physician / laboratory rep: _____

Name of diagnostic test: _____

_____

Reason for test: _____

_____

Prep for test: _____

_____

Results of test: _____

_____

_____

_____

_____

Date: _____ Test ordered by: _____

Name of laboratory / hospital / facility: _____

Name of attending physician / laboratory rep: _____

Name of diagnostic test: _____

_____

Reason for test: _____

_____

Prep for test: _____

_____

Results of test: _____

_____

_____

_____

Date: _____

Doctor's name: _____

Facility name / Phone: _____

Reason for visit: _____

Symptoms: _____

_____

_____

_____

Questions: _____

_____

_____

_____

Doctor's advice/Procedure performed: _____

_____

_____

_____

_____

Plan of action: _____

_____

_____

Prescribed medications: _____

_____

Follow up required: _____

_____

_____

_____

_____

_____

Weight: _____ Blood Pressure: _____ Heart Rate: _____ Temp: _____

Prescribed Diagnostic Tests

Date: _____ Test ordered by: _____

Name of laboratory / hospital / facility: _____

Name of attending physician / laboratory rep: _____

Name of diagnostic test: _____

_____

Reason for test: _____

_____

Prep for test: _____

_____

Results of test: _____

_____

_____

_____

Date: _____ Test ordered by: _____

Name of laboratory / hospital / facility: _____

Name of attending physician / laboratory rep: _____

Name of diagnostic test: _____

_____

Reason for test: _____

_____

Prep for test: _____

_____

Results of test: _____

_____

_____

_____

Date: _____

Doctor's name: _____

Facility name / Phone: _____

Reason for visit: _____

Symptoms: _____

_____

_____

_____

Questions: _____

_____

_____

Doctor's advice/Procedure performed: _____

_____

_____

_____

_____

Plan of action: _____

_____

_____

Prescribed medications: _____

_____

Follow up required: _____

_____

_____

_____

_____

Weight: _____ Blood Pressure: _____ Heart Rate: _____ Temp: _____

Prescribed Diagnostic Tests

Date: _____ Test ordered by: _____

Name of laboratory / hospital / facility: _____

Name of attending physician / laboratory rep: _____

Name of diagnostic test: _____

_____

Reason for test: _____

_____

Prep for test: _____

_____

Results of test: _____

_____

_____

_____

_____

Date: _____ Test ordered by: _____

Name of laboratory / hospital / facility: _____

Name of attending physician / laboratory rep: _____

Name of diagnostic test: _____

_____

Reason for test: _____

_____

Prep for test: _____

_____

Results of test: _____

_____

_____

_____

Date: _____

Doctor's name: _____

Facility name / Phone: _____

Reason for visit: _____

_____

Symptoms: _____

_____

_____

_____

Questions: _____

_____

_____

Doctor's advice/Procedure performed: _____

_____

_____

_____

_____

_____

Plan of action: _____

_____

_____

Prescribed medications: _____

_____

Follow up required: _____

_____

_____

_____

_____

_____

Weight: _____ Blood Pressure: _____ Heart Rate: _____ Temp: _____

Prescribed Diagnostic Tests

Date: _____ Test ordered by: _____

Name of laboratory / hospital / facility: _____

Name of attending physician / laboratory rep: _____

Name of diagnostic test: _____

_____

Reason for test: _____

_____

Prep for test: _____

_____

Results of test: _____

_____

_____

_____

_____

Date: _____ Test ordered by: _____

Name of laboratory / hospital / facility: _____

Name of attending physician / laboratory rep: _____

Name of diagnostic test: _____

_____

Reason for test: _____

_____

Prep for test: _____

_____

Results of test: _____

_____

_____

_____

Date: _____

Doctor's name: _____

Facility name / Phone: _____

Reason for visit: _____

_____

Symptoms: _____

_____

_____

_____

Questions: _____

_____

_____

_____

Doctor's advice/Procedure performed: _____

_____

_____

_____

_____

Plan of action: _____

_____

_____

Prescribed medications: _____

_____

Follow up required: _____

_____

_____

_____

_____

_____

Weight: _____ Blood Pressure: _____ Heart Rate: _____ Temp: _____

Prescribed Diagnostic Tests

Date: _____ Test ordered by:_____

Name of laboratory / hospital / facility: _____

Name of attending physician / laboratory rep:_____

Name of diagnostic test:_____

_____

Reason for test:_____

_____

Prep for test: _____

_____

Results of test: _____

_____

_____

_____

_____

Date: _____ Test ordered by:_____

Name of laboratory / hospital / facility: _____

Name of attending physician / laboratory rep:_____

Name of diagnostic test:_____

_____

Reason for test:_____

_____

Prep for test: _____

_____

Results of test: _____

_____

_____

_____

Date: _____

Doctor's name: _____

Facility name / Phone: _____

Reason for visit: _____

Symptoms: _____

_____

_____

_____

Questions: _____

_____

_____

Doctor's advice/Procedure performed: _____

_____

_____

_____

_____

_____

Plan of action: _____

_____

_____

Prescribed medications: _____

_____

Follow up required: _____

_____

_____

_____

_____

Weight: _____ Blood Pressure: _____ Heart Rate: _____ Temp: _____

Prescribed Diagnostic Tests

Date: _____ Test ordered by:_____

Name of laboratory / hospital / facility: _____

Name of attending physician / laboratory rep:_____

Name of diagnostic test: _____

_____

Reason for test:_____

_____

Prep for test: _____

_____

Results of test: _____

_____

_____

_____

Date: _____ Test ordered by:_____

Name of laboratory / hospital / facility: _____

Name of attending physician / laboratory rep:_____

Name of diagnostic test: _____

_____

Reason for test:_____

_____

Prep for test: _____

_____

Results of test: _____

_____

_____

_____

Date: _____

Doctor's name: _____

Facility name / Phone: _____

Reason for visit: _____

Symptoms: _____
_____
_____
_____

Questions: _____
_____
_____

Doctor's advice/Procedure performed: _____
_____
_____
_____
_____

Plan of action: _____
_____
_____

Prescribed medications: _____
_____

Follow up required: _____
_____
_____
_____
_____

Weight: _____ Blood Pressure: _____ Heart Rate: _____ Temp: _____

Prescribed Diagnostic Tests

Date: _____ Test ordered by: _____

Name of laboratory / hospital / facility: _____

Name of attending physician / laboratory rep: _____

Name of diagnostic test: _____

_____

Reason for test: _____

_____

Prep for test: _____

Results of test: _____

_____

_____

_____

Date: _____ Test ordered by: _____

Name of laboratory / hospital / facility: _____

Name of attending physician / laboratory rep: _____

Name of diagnostic test: _____

_____

Reason for test: _____

_____

Prep for test: _____

Results of test: _____

_____

_____

_____

Date: _____

Doctor's name: _____

Facility name / Phone: _____

Reason for visit: _____

_____

Symptoms: _____

_____

_____

_____

Questions: _____

_____

_____

Doctor's advice/Procedure performed: _____

_____

_____

_____

_____

_____

Plan of action: _____

_____

_____

Prescribed medications: _____

_____

Follow up required: _____

_____

_____

_____

_____

_____

Weight: _____ Blood Pressure: _____ Heart Rate: _____ Temp: _____

Prescribed Diagnostic Tests

Date: _____ Test ordered by: _____

Name of laboratory / hospital / facility: _____

Name of attending physician / laboratory rep: _____

Name of diagnostic test: _____

_____

Reason for test: _____

_____

Prep for test: _____

_____

Results of test: _____

_____

_____

_____

Date: _____ Test ordered by: _____

Name of laboratory / hospital / facility: _____

Name of attending physician / laboratory rep: _____

Name of diagnostic test: _____

_____

Reason for test: _____

_____

Prep for test: _____

_____

Results of test: _____

_____

_____

_____

Date: _____

Doctor's name: _____

Facility name / Phone: _____

Reason for visit: _____

_____

Symptoms: _____

_____

_____

_____

Questions: _____

_____

_____

Doctor's advice/Procedure performed: _____

_____

_____

_____

_____

Plan of action: _____

_____

_____

Prescribed medications: _____

_____

Follow up required: _____

_____

_____

_____

_____

_____

Weight: _____ Blood Pressure: _____ Heart Rate: _____ Temp: _____

Prescribed Diagnostic Tests

Date: _____ Test ordered by: _____

Name of laboratory / hospital / facility: _____

Name of attending physician / laboratory rep: _____

Name of diagnostic test: _____

_____

Reason for test: _____

_____

Prep for test: _____

_____

Results of test: _____

_____

_____

_____

_____

Date: _____ Test ordered by: _____

Name of laboratory / hospital / facility: _____

Name of attending physician / laboratory rep: _____

Name of diagnostic test: _____

_____

Reason for test: _____

_____

Prep for test: _____

_____

Results of test: _____

_____

_____

_____

Date: _____

Doctor's name: _____

Facility name / Phone: _____

Reason for visit: _____

_____

Symptoms: _____

_____

_____

_____

Questions: _____

_____

_____

_____

Doctor's advice/Procedure performed: _____

_____

_____

_____

_____

_____

Plan of action: _____

_____

_____

Prescribed medications: _____

_____

Follow up required: _____

_____

_____

_____

_____

_____

Weight: _____ Blood Pressure: _____ Heart Rate: _____ Temp: _____

Prescribed Diagnostic Tests

Date: _____ Test ordered by: _____

Name of laboratory / hospital / facility: _____

Name of attending physician / laboratory rep: _____

Name of diagnostic test: _____

_____

Reason for test: _____

_____

Prep for test: _____

_____

Results of test: _____

_____

_____

_____

Date: _____ Test ordered by: _____

Name of laboratory / hospital / facility: _____

Name of attending physician / laboratory rep: _____

Name of diagnostic test: _____

_____

Reason for test: _____

_____

Prep for test: _____

_____

Results of test: _____

_____

_____

_____

Date: _____

Doctor's name: _____

Facility name / Phone: _____

Reason for visit: _____

_____

Symptoms: _____

_____

_____

_____

Questions: _____

_____

_____

Doctor's advice/Procedure performed: _____

_____

_____

_____

_____

_____

Plan of action: _____

_____

_____

Prescribed medications: _____

_____

Follow up required: _____

_____

_____

_____

_____

_____

Weight: _____ Blood Pressure: _____ Heart Rate: _____ Temp: _____

Prescribed Diagnostic Tests

Date: _____ Test ordered by: _____

Name of laboratory / hospital / facility: _____

Name of attending physician / laboratory rep: _____

Name of diagnostic test: _____

_____

Reason for test: _____

_____

Prep for test: _____

_____

Results of test: _____

_____

_____

_____

Date: _____ Test ordered by: _____

Name of laboratory / hospital / facility: _____

Name of attending physician / laboratory rep: _____

Name of diagnostic test: _____

_____

Reason for test: _____

_____

Prep for test: _____

_____

Results of test: _____

_____

_____

_____

Date: _____

Doctor's name: _____

Facility name / Phone: _____

Reason for visit: _____
_____

Symptoms: _____
_____
_____
_____

Questions: _____
_____
_____

Doctor's advice/Procedure performed: _____
_____
_____
_____
_____
_____

Plan of action: _____
_____
_____

Prescribed medications: _____
_____

Follow up required: _____
_____
_____
_____
_____

Weight: _____ Blood Pressure: _____ Heart Rate: _____ Temp: _____

Prescribed Diagnostic Tests

Date: _____ Test ordered by: _____

Name of laboratory / hospital / facility: _____

Name of attending physician / laboratory rep: _____

Name of diagnostic test: _____

_____

Reason for test: _____

_____

Prep for test: _____

_____

Results of test: _____

_____

_____

_____

Date: _____ Test ordered by: _____

Name of laboratory / hospital / facility: _____

Name of attending physician / laboratory rep: _____

Name of diagnostic test: _____

_____

Reason for test: _____

_____

Prep for test: _____

_____

Results of test: _____

_____

_____

_____

Date: _____

Doctor's name: _____

Facility name / Phone: _____

Reason for visit: _____

Symptoms: _____

_____

_____

_____

Questions: _____

_____

_____

Doctor's advice/Procedure performed: _____

_____

_____

_____

_____

_____

Plan of action: _____

_____

_____

Prescribed medications: _____

_____

Follow up required: _____

_____

_____

_____

_____

_____

Weight: _____ Blood Pressure: _____ Heart Rate: _____ Temp: _____

Prescribed Diagnostic Tests

Date: _____ Test ordered by: _____

Name of laboratory / hospital / facility: _____

Name of attending physician / laboratory rep: _____

Name of diagnostic test: _____

_____

Reason for test: _____

_____

Prep for test: _____

_____

Results of test: _____

_____

_____

_____

Date: _____ Test ordered by: _____

Name of laboratory / hospital / facility: _____

Name of attending physician / laboratory rep: _____

Name of diagnostic test: _____

_____

Reason for test: _____

_____

Prep for test: _____

_____

Results of test: _____

_____

_____

_____

Date: _____

Doctor's name: _____

Facility name / Phone: _____

Reason for visit: _____

Symptoms: _____

_____

_____

_____

Questions: _____

_____

_____

Doctor's advice/Procedure performed: _____

_____

_____

_____

_____

_____

Plan of action: _____

_____

_____

Prescribed medications: _____

_____

Follow up required: _____

_____

_____

_____

_____

_____

Weight: _____ Blood Pressure: _____ Heart Rate: _____ Temp: _____

Prescribed Diagnostic Tests

Date: _____ Test ordered by:_____

Name of laboratory / hospital / facility: _____

Name of attending physician / laboratory rep:_____

Name of diagnostic test:_____

_____

Reason for test:_____

_____

Prep for test: _____

_____

Results of test: _____

_____

_____

_____

Date: _____ Test ordered by:_____

Name of laboratory / hospital / facility: _____

Name of attending physician / laboratory rep:_____

Name of diagnostic test:_____

_____

Reason for test:_____

_____

Prep for test: _____

_____

Results of test: _____

_____

_____

_____

Date: _____

Doctor's name: _____

Facility name / Phone: _____

Reason for visit: _____

_____

Symptoms: _____

_____

_____

_____

Questions: _____

_____

_____

Doctor's advice/Procedure performed: _____

_____

_____

_____

_____

Plan of action: _____

_____

_____

Prescribed medications: _____

_____

Follow up required: _____

_____

_____

_____

_____

Weight: _____ Blood Pressure: _____ Heart Rate: _____ Temp: _____

Prescribed Diagnostic Tests

Date: _____ Test ordered by: _____

Name of laboratory / hospital / facility: _____

Name of attending physician / laboratory rep: _____

Name of diagnostic test: _____

_____

Reason for test: _____

_____

Prep for test: _____

_____

Results of test: _____

_____

_____

_____

_____

Date: _____ Test ordered by: _____

Name of laboratory / hospital / facility: _____

Name of attending physician / laboratory rep: _____

Name of diagnostic test: _____

_____

Reason for test: _____

_____

Prep for test: _____

_____

Results of test: _____

_____

_____

_____

Date: _____

Doctor's name: _____

Facility name / Phone: _____

Reason for visit: _____

Symptoms: _____

_____

_____

_____

Questions: _____

_____

_____

Doctor's advice/Procedure performed: _____

_____

_____

_____

_____

_____

Plan of action: _____

_____

_____

Prescribed medications: _____

_____

Follow up required: _____

_____

_____

_____

_____

_____

Weight: _____ Blood Pressure: _____ Heart Rate: _____ Temp: _____

Prescribed Diagnostic Tests

Date: _____ Test ordered by: _____

Name of laboratory / hospital / facility: _____

Name of attending physician / laboratory rep: _____

Name of diagnostic test: _____

_____

Reason for test: _____

_____

Prep for test: _____

_____

Results of test: _____

_____

_____

_____

_____

Date: _____ Test ordered by: _____

Name of laboratory / hospital / facility: _____

Name of attending physician / laboratory rep: _____

Name of diagnostic test: _____

_____

Reason for test: _____

_____

Prep for test: _____

_____

Results of test: _____

_____

_____

_____

_____

Date: _____

Doctor's name: _____

Facility name / Phone: _____

Reason for visit: _____

Symptoms: _____

_____

_____

_____

Questions: _____

_____

_____

Doctor's advice/Procedure performed: _____

_____

_____

_____

_____

_____

Plan of action: _____

_____

_____

Prescribed medications: _____

_____

Follow up required: _____

_____

_____

_____

_____

_____

Weight: _____ Blood Pressure: _____ Heart Rate: _____ Temp: _____

Prescribed Diagnostic Tests

Date: _____ Test ordered by: _____

Name of laboratory / hospital / facility: _____

Name of attending physician / laboratory rep: _____

Name of diagnostic test: _____

_____

Reason for test: _____

_____

Prep for test: _____

_____

Results of test: _____

_____

_____

_____

Date: _____ Test ordered by: _____

Name of laboratory / hospital / facility: _____

Name of attending physician / laboratory rep: _____

Name of diagnostic test: _____

_____

Reason for test: _____

_____

Prep for test: _____

_____

Results of test: _____

_____

_____

_____

Date: _____

Doctor's name: _____

Facility name / Phone: _____

Reason for visit: _____

Symptoms: _____
_____
_____
_____

Questions: _____
_____
_____

Doctor's advice/Procedure performed: _____
_____
_____
_____
_____

Plan of action: _____
_____
_____

Prescribed medications: _____
_____

Follow up required: _____
_____
_____
_____
_____
_____

Weight: _____ Blood Pressure: _____ Heart Rate: _____ Temp: _____

Prescribed Diagnostic Tests

Date: _____ Test ordered by: _____

Name of laboratory / hospital / facility: _____

Name of attending physician / laboratory rep: _____

Name of diagnostic test: _____

_____

Reason for test: _____

_____

Prep for test: _____

_____

Results of test: _____

_____

_____

_____

_____

Date: _____ Test ordered by: _____

Name of laboratory / hospital / facility: _____

Name of attending physician / laboratory rep: _____

Name of diagnostic test: _____

_____

Reason for test: _____

_____

Prep for test: _____

_____

Results of test: _____

_____

_____

_____

Date: _____

Doctor's name: _____

Facility name / Phone: _____

Reason for visit: _____

_____

Symptoms: _____

_____

_____

_____

Questions: _____

_____

_____

_____

Doctor's advice/Procedure performed: _____

_____

_____

_____

_____

_____

Plan of action: _____

_____

_____

Prescribed medications: _____

_____

Follow up required: _____

_____

_____

_____

_____

_____

Weight: _____ Blood Pressure: _____ Heart Rate: _____ Temp: _____

Prescribed Diagnostic Tests

Date: _____ Test ordered by:_____

Name of laboratory / hospital / facility: _____

Name of attending physician / laboratory rep:_____

Name of diagnostic test: _____

_____

Reason for test:_____

_____

Prep for test: _____

_____

Results of test: _____

_____

_____

_____

Date: _____ Test ordered by:_____

Name of laboratory / hospital / facility: _____

Name of attending physician / laboratory rep:_____

Name of diagnostic test: _____

_____

Reason for test:_____

_____

Prep for test: _____

_____

Results of test: _____

_____

_____

_____

Date: _____

Doctor's name: _____

Facility name / Phone: _____

Reason for visit: _____

Symptoms: _____
_____
_____
_____

Questions: _____
_____
_____

Doctor's advice/Procedure performed: _____
_____
_____
_____
_____

Plan of action: _____
_____
_____

Prescribed medications: _____
_____

Follow up required: _____
_____
_____
_____
_____

Weight: _____ Blood Pressure: _____ Heart Rate: _____ Temp: _____

Prescribed Diagnostic Tests

Date: _____ Test ordered by: _____

Name of laboratory / hospital / facility: _____

Name of attending physician / laboratory rep: _____

Name of diagnostic test: _____

_____

Reason for test: _____

_____

Prep for test: _____

_____

Results of test: _____

_____

_____

_____

Date: _____ Test ordered by: _____

Name of laboratory / hospital / facility: _____

Name of attending physician / laboratory rep: _____

Name of diagnostic test: _____

_____

Reason for test: _____

_____

Prep for test: _____

_____

Results of test: _____

_____

_____

_____

Date: _____

Doctor's name: _____

Facility name / Phone: _____

Reason for visit: _____

_____

Symptoms: _____

_____

_____

_____

Questions: _____

_____

_____

Doctor's advice/Procedure performed: _____

_____

_____

_____

_____

_____

Plan of action: _____

_____

_____

Prescribed medications: _____

_____

Follow up required: _____

_____

_____

_____

_____

_____

Weight: _____ Blood Pressure: _____ Heart Rate: _____ Temp: _____

Prescribed Diagnostic Tests

Date: _____ Test ordered by: _____

Name of laboratory / hospital / facility: _____

Name of attending physician / laboratory rep: _____

Name of diagnostic test: _____

_____

Reason for test: _____

_____

Prep for test: _____

_____

Results of test: _____

_____

_____

_____

_____

Date: _____ Test ordered by: _____

Name of laboratory / hospital / facility: _____

Name of attending physician / laboratory rep: _____

Name of diagnostic test: _____

_____

Reason for test: _____

_____

Prep for test: _____

_____

Results of test: _____

_____

_____

_____

Date: _____

Doctor's name: _____

Facility name / Phone: _____

Reason for visit: _____

Symptoms: _____

_____

_____

_____

Questions: _____

_____

_____

Doctor's advice/Procedure performed: _____

_____

_____

_____

_____

_____

Plan of action: _____

_____

_____

Prescribed medications: _____

_____

Follow up required: _____

_____

_____

_____

_____

_____

Weight: _____ Blood Pressure: _____ Heart Rate: _____ Temp: _____

Prescribed Diagnostic Tests

Date: _____ Test ordered by: _____

Name of laboratory / hospital / facility: _____

Name of attending physician / laboratory rep: _____

Name of diagnostic test: _____

_____

Reason for test: _____

_____

Prep for test: _____

_____

Results of test: _____

_____

_____

_____

Date: _____ Test ordered by: _____

Name of laboratory / hospital / facility: _____

Name of attending physician / laboratory rep: _____

Name of diagnostic test: _____

_____

Reason for test: _____

_____

Prep for test: _____

_____

Results of test: _____

_____

_____

_____

Date: _____

Doctor's name: _____

Facility name / Phone: _____

Reason for visit: _____

_____

Symptoms: _____

_____

_____

_____

Questions: _____

_____

_____

Doctor's advice/Procedure performed: _____

_____

_____

_____

_____

_____

Plan of action: _____

_____

_____

Prescribed medications: _____

_____

Follow up required: _____

_____

_____

_____

_____

_____

Weight: _____ Blood Pressure: _____ Heart Rate: _____ Temp: _____

Prescribed Diagnostic Tests

Date: _____ Test ordered by: _____

Name of laboratory / hospital / facility: _____

Name of attending physician / laboratory rep: _____

Name of diagnostic test: _____

_____

Reason for test: _____

_____

Prep for test: _____

_____

Results of test: _____

_____

_____

_____

Date: _____ Test ordered by: _____

Name of laboratory / hospital / facility: _____

Name of attending physician / laboratory rep: _____

Name of diagnostic test: _____

_____

Reason for test: _____

_____

Prep for test: _____

_____

Results of test: _____

_____

_____

_____

Date: _____

Doctor's name: _____

Facility name / Phone: _____

Reason for visit: _____

Symptoms: _____
_____
_____
_____

Questions: _____
_____
_____

Doctor's advice/Procedure performed: _____
_____
_____
_____
_____
_____

Plan of action: _____
_____
_____

Prescribed medications: _____
_____

Follow up required: _____
_____
_____
_____
_____

Weight: _____ Blood Pressure: _____ Heart Rate: _____ Temp: _____

Prescribed Diagnostic Tests

Date: _____ Test ordered by: _____

Name of laboratory / hospital / facility: _____

Name of attending physician / laboratory rep: _____

Name of diagnostic test: _____

_____

Reason for test: _____

_____

Prep for test: _____

Results of test: _____

_____

_____

_____

Date: _____ Test ordered by: _____

Name of laboratory / hospital / facility: _____

Name of attending physician / laboratory rep: _____

Name of diagnostic test: _____

_____

Reason for test: _____

_____

Prep for test: _____

Results of test: _____

_____

_____

_____

Date: _____

Doctor's name: _____

Facility name / Phone: _____

Reason for visit: _____

_____

Symptoms: _____

_____

_____

_____

Questions: _____

_____

_____

Doctor's advice/Procedure performed: _____

_____

_____

_____

_____

_____

Plan of action: _____

_____

_____

Prescribed medications: _____

_____

Follow up required: _____

_____

_____

_____

_____

_____

Weight: _____ Blood Pressure: _____ Heart Rate: _____ Temp: _____

Prescribed Diagnostic Tests

Date: _____ Test ordered by: _____

Name of laboratory / hospital / facility: _____

Name of attending physician / laboratory rep: _____

Name of diagnostic test: _____

_____

Reason for test: _____

_____

Prep for test: _____

_____

Results of test: _____

_____

_____

_____

Date: _____ Test ordered by: _____

Name of laboratory / hospital / facility: _____

Name of attending physician / laboratory rep: _____

Name of diagnostic test: _____

_____

Reason for test: _____

_____

Prep for test: _____

_____

Results of test: _____

_____

_____

_____

Date: _____

Doctor's name: _____

Facility name / Phone: _____

Reason for visit: _____
_____

Symptoms: _____
_____
_____
_____

Questions: _____
_____
_____

Doctor's advice/Procedure performed: _____
_____
_____
_____
_____

Plan of action: _____
_____
_____

Prescribed medications: _____
_____

Follow up required: _____
_____
_____
_____
_____
_____

Weight: _____ Blood Pressure: _____ Heart Rate: _____ Temp: _____

Prescribed Diagnostic Tests

Date: _____ Test ordered by: _____

Name of laboratory / hospital / facility: _____

Name of attending physician / laboratory rep: _____

Name of diagnostic test: _____

_____

Reason for test: _____

_____

Prep for test: _____

_____

Results of test: _____

_____

_____

_____

_____

Date: _____ Test ordered by: _____

Name of laboratory / hospital / facility: _____

Name of attending physician / laboratory rep: _____

Name of diagnostic test: _____

_____

Reason for test: _____

_____

Prep for test: _____

_____

Results of test: _____

_____

_____

_____

Date: _____

Doctor's name: _____

Facility name / Phone: _____

Reason for visit: _____

_____

Symptoms: _____

_____

_____

_____

Questions: _____

_____

_____

Doctor's advice/Procedure performed: _____

_____

_____

_____

_____

Plan of action: _____

_____

_____

Prescribed medications: _____

_____

Follow up required: _____

_____

_____

_____

_____

_____

Weight: _____ Blood Pressure: _____ Heart Rate: _____ Temp: _____

Prescribed Diagnostic Tests

Date: _____ Test ordered by: _____

Name of laboratory / hospital / facility: _____

Name of attending physician / laboratory rep: _____

Name of diagnostic test: _____

_____

Reason for test: _____

_____

Prep for test: _____

_____

Results of test: _____

_____

_____

_____

Date: _____ Test ordered by: _____

Name of laboratory / hospital / facility: _____

Name of attending physician / laboratory rep: _____

Name of diagnostic test: _____

_____

Reason for test: _____

_____

Prep for test: _____

_____

Results of test: _____

_____

_____

_____

Date: _____

Doctor's name: _____

Facility name / Phone: _____

Reason for visit: _____

Symptoms: _____

_____

_____

_____

Questions: _____

_____

_____

Doctor's advice/Procedure performed: _____

_____

_____

_____

_____

Plan of action: _____

_____

_____

Prescribed medications: _____

_____

Follow up required: _____

_____

_____

_____

_____

Weight: _____ Blood Pressure: _____ Heart Rate: _____ Temp: _____

Prescribed Diagnostic Tests

Date: _____ Test ordered by: _____

Name of laboratory / hospital / facility: _____

Name of attending physician / laboratory rep: _____

Name of diagnostic test: _____

_____

Reason for test: _____

_____

Prep for test: _____

_____

Results of test: _____

_____

_____

_____

_____

Date: _____ Test ordered by: _____

Name of laboratory / hospital / facility: _____

Name of attending physician / laboratory rep: _____

Name of diagnostic test: _____

_____

Reason for test: _____

_____

Prep for test: _____

_____

Results of test: _____

_____

_____

_____

Date: _____

Doctor's name: _____

Facility name / Phone: _____

Reason for visit: _____

_____

Symptoms: _____

_____

_____

_____

Questions: _____

_____

_____

Doctor's advice/Procedure performed: _____

_____

_____

_____

_____

_____

Plan of action: _____

_____

_____

Prescribed medications: _____

_____

Follow up required: _____

_____

_____

_____

_____

_____

Weight: _____ Blood Pressure: _____ Heart Rate: _____ Temp: _____

Prescribed Diagnostic Tests

Date: _____ Test ordered by: _____

Name of laboratory / hospital / facility: _____

Name of attending physician / laboratory rep: _____

Name of diagnostic test: _____

_____

Reason for test: _____

_____

Prep for test: _____

_____

Results of test: _____

_____

_____

_____

Date: _____ Test ordered by: _____

Name of laboratory / hospital / facility: _____

Name of attending physician / laboratory rep: _____

Name of diagnostic test: _____

_____

Reason for test: _____

_____

Prep for test: _____

_____

Results of test: _____

_____

_____

_____

Date: _____

Doctor's name: _____

Facility name / Phone: _____

Reason for visit: _____

Symptoms: _____

_____

_____

_____

Questions: _____

_____

_____

Doctor's advice/Procedure performed: _____

_____

_____

_____

_____

_____

Plan of action: _____

_____

_____

Prescribed medications: _____

_____

Follow up required: _____

_____

_____

_____

_____

_____

Weight: _____ Blood Pressure: _____ Heart Rate: _____ Temp: _____

Prescribed Diagnostic Tests

Date: _____ Test ordered by: _____

Name of laboratory / hospital / facility: _____

Name of attending physician / laboratory rep: _____

Name of diagnostic test: _____

_____

Reason for test: _____

_____

Prep for test: _____

_____

Results of test: _____

_____

_____

_____

Date: _____ Test ordered by: _____

Name of laboratory / hospital / facility: _____

Name of attending physician / laboratory rep: _____

Name of diagnostic test: _____

_____

Reason for test: _____

_____

Prep for test: _____

_____

Results of test: _____

_____

_____

_____

Date: _____

Doctor's name: _____

Facility name / Phone: _____

Reason for visit: _____

Symptoms: _____

_____

_____

_____

Questions: _____

_____

_____

Doctor's advice/Procedure performed: _____

_____

_____

_____

_____

_____

Plan of action: _____

_____

_____

Prescribed medications: _____

_____

Follow up required: _____

_____

_____

_____

_____

_____

Weight: _____ Blood Pressure: _____ Heart Rate: _____ Temp: _____

Prescribed Diagnostic Tests

Date: _____ Test ordered by: _____

Name of laboratory / hospital / facility: _____

Name of attending physician / laboratory rep: _____

Name of diagnostic test: _____

_____

Reason for test: _____

_____

Prep for test: _____

_____

Results of test: _____

_____

_____

_____

_____

Date: _____ Test ordered by: _____

Name of laboratory / hospital / facility: _____

Name of attending physician / laboratory rep: _____

Name of diagnostic test: _____

_____

Reason for test: _____

_____

Prep for test: _____

_____

Results of test: _____

_____

_____

_____

Date: _____

Doctor's name: _____

Facility name / Phone: _____

Reason for visit: _____

Symptoms: _____
_____
_____
_____

Questions: _____
_____
_____

Doctor's advice/Procedure performed: _____
_____
_____
_____
_____

Plan of action: _____
_____
_____

Prescribed medications: _____
_____

Follow up required: _____
_____
_____
_____
_____

Weight: _____ Blood Pressure: _____ Heart Rate: _____ Temp: _____

Prescribed Diagnostic Tests

Date: _____ Test ordered by: _____

Name of laboratory / hospital / facility: _____

Name of attending physician / laboratory rep: _____

Name of diagnostic test: _____

_____

Reason for test: _____

_____

Prep for test: _____

Results of test: _____

_____

_____

_____

_____

Date: _____ Test ordered by: _____

Name of laboratory / hospital / facility: _____

Name of attending physician / laboratory rep: _____

Name of diagnostic test: _____

_____

Reason for test: _____

_____

Prep for test: _____

Results of test: _____

_____

_____

_____

Date: _____

Doctor's name: _____

Facility name / Phone: _____

Reason for visit: _____

_____

Symptoms: _____

_____

_____

_____

Questions: _____

_____

_____

Doctor's advice/Procedure performed: _____

_____

_____

_____

_____

_____

Plan of action: _____

_____

_____

Prescribed medications: _____

_____

Follow up required: _____

_____

_____

_____

_____

_____

Weight: _____ Blood Pressure: _____ Heart Rate: _____ Temp: _____

Prescribed Diagnostic Tests

Date: _____ Test ordered by:_____

Name of laboratory / hospital / facility: _____

Name of attending physician / laboratory rep:_____

Name of diagnostic test: _____

_____

Reason for test:_____

_____

Prep for test: _____

_____

Results of test: _____

_____

_____

_____

_____

Date: _____ Test ordered by:_____

Name of laboratory / hospital / facility: _____

Name of attending physician / laboratory rep:_____

Name of diagnostic test: _____

_____

Reason for test:_____

_____

Prep for test: _____

_____

Results of test: _____

_____

_____

_____

Date: _____

Doctor's name: _____

Facility name / Phone: _____

Reason for visit: _____

_____

Symptoms: _____

_____

_____

_____

Questions: _____

_____

_____

Doctor's advice/Procedure performed: _____

_____

_____

_____

_____

_____

Plan of action: _____

_____

_____

Prescribed medications: _____

_____

Follow up required: _____

_____

_____

_____

_____

_____

Weight: _____ Blood Pressure: _____ Heart Rate: _____ Temp: _____

Prescribed Diagnostic Tests

Date: _____ Test ordered by:_____

Name of laboratory / hospital / facility: _____

Name of attending physician / laboratory rep:_____

Name of diagnostic test:_____

_____

Reason for test:_____

_____

Prep for test: _____

_____

Results of test: _____

_____

_____

_____

Date: _____ Test ordered by:_____

Name of laboratory / hospital / facility: _____

Name of attending physician / laboratory rep:_____

Name of diagnostic test:_____

_____

Reason for test:_____

_____

Prep for test: _____

_____

Results of test: _____

_____

_____

_____

Date: _____

Doctor's name: _____

Facility name / Phone: _____

Reason for visit: _____

_____

Symptoms: _____

_____

_____

_____

Questions: _____

_____

_____

Doctor's advice/Procedure performed: _____

_____

_____

_____

_____

Plan of action: _____

_____

_____

Prescribed medications: _____

_____

Follow up required: _____

_____

_____

_____

_____

Weight: _____ Blood Pressure: _____ Heart Rate: _____ Temp: _____

Prescribed Diagnostic Tests

Date: _____ Test ordered by: _____

Name of laboratory / hospital / facility: _____

Name of attending physician / laboratory rep: _____

Name of diagnostic test: _____

_____

Reason for test: _____

_____

Prep for test: _____

_____

Results of test: _____

_____

_____

_____

_____

Date: _____ Test ordered by: _____

Name of laboratory / hospital / facility: _____

Name of attending physician / laboratory rep: _____

Name of diagnostic test: _____

_____

Reason for test: _____

_____

Prep for test: _____

_____

Results of test: _____

_____

_____

_____

Date: _____

Doctor's name: _____

Facility name / Phone: _____

Reason for visit: _____

_____

Symptoms: _____

_____

_____

_____

Questions: _____

_____

_____

Doctor's advice/Procedure performed: _____

_____

_____

_____

_____

_____

Plan of action: _____

_____

_____

Prescribed medications: _____

_____

Follow up required: _____

_____

_____

_____

_____

_____

Weight: _____ Blood Pressure: _____ Heart Rate: _____ Temp: _____

Prescribed Diagnostic Tests

Date: _____ Test ordered by: _____

Name of laboratory / hospital / facility: _____

Name of attending physician / laboratory rep: _____

Name of diagnostic test: _____

_____

Reason for test: _____

_____

Prep for test: _____

Results of test: _____

_____

_____

_____

Date: _____ Test ordered by: _____

Name of laboratory / hospital / facility: _____

Name of attending physician / laboratory rep: _____

Name of diagnostic test: _____

_____

Reason for test: _____

_____

Prep for test: _____

Results of test: _____

_____

_____

_____

Date: _____

Doctor's name: _____

Facility name / Phone: _____

Reason for visit: _____

Symptoms: _____

_____

_____

_____

Questions: _____

_____

_____

Doctor's advice/Procedure performed: _____

_____

_____

_____

_____

_____

Plan of action: _____

_____

_____

Prescribed medications: _____

_____

Follow up required: _____

_____

_____

_____

_____

_____

Weight: _____ Blood Pressure: _____ Heart Rate: _____ Temp: _____

Prescribed Diagnostic Tests

Date: _____ Test ordered by: _____

Name of laboratory / hospital / facility: _____

Name of attending physician / laboratory rep: _____

Name of diagnostic test: _____

_____

Reason for test: _____

_____

Prep for test: _____

_____

Results of test: _____

_____

_____

_____

_____

Date: _____ Test ordered by: _____

Name of laboratory / hospital / facility: _____

Name of attending physician / laboratory rep: _____

Name of diagnostic test: _____

_____

Reason for test: _____

_____

Prep for test: _____

_____

Results of test: _____

_____

_____

_____

Date: _____

Doctor's name: _____

Facility name / Phone: _____

Reason for visit: _____

Symptoms: _____

_____

_____

_____

Questions: _____

_____

_____

Doctor's advice/Procedure performed: _____

_____

_____

_____

_____

Plan of action: _____

_____

_____

Prescribed medications: _____

_____

Follow up required: _____

_____

_____

_____

_____

_____

Weight: _____ Blood Pressure: _____ Heart Rate: _____ Temp: _____

Prescribed Diagnostic Tests

Date: _____ Test ordered by: _____

Name of laboratory / hospital / facility: _____

Name of attending physician / laboratory rep: _____

Name of diagnostic test: _____

_____

Reason for test: _____

_____

Prep for test: _____

_____

Results of test: _____

_____

_____

_____

_____

Date: _____ Test ordered by: _____

Name of laboratory / hospital / facility: _____

Name of attending physician / laboratory rep: _____

Name of diagnostic test: _____

_____

Reason for test: _____

_____

Prep for test: _____

_____

Results of test: _____

_____

_____

_____

Date: _____

Doctor's name: _____

Facility name / Phone: _____

Reason for visit: _____

_____

Symptoms: _____

_____

_____

_____

Questions: _____

_____

_____

Doctor's advice/Procedure performed: _____

_____

_____

_____

_____

_____

Plan of action: _____

_____

_____

Prescribed medications: _____

_____

Follow up required: _____

_____

_____

_____

_____

_____

Weight: _____ Blood Pressure: _____ Heart Rate: _____ Temp: _____

Prescribed Diagnostic Tests

Date: _____ Test ordered by: _____

Name of laboratory / hospital / facility: _____

Name of attending physician / laboratory rep: _____

Name of diagnostic test: _____

_____

Reason for test: _____

_____

Prep for test: _____

_____

Results of test: _____

_____

_____

_____

Date: _____ Test ordered by: _____

Name of laboratory / hospital / facility: _____

Name of attending physician / laboratory rep: _____

Name of diagnostic test: _____

_____

Reason for test: _____

_____

Prep for test: _____

_____

Results of test: _____

_____

_____

_____

Date: _____

Doctor's name: _____

Facility name / Phone: _____

Reason for visit: _____

Symptoms: _____
_____
_____
_____

Questions: _____
_____
_____

Doctor's advice/Procedure performed: _____
_____
_____
_____
_____

Plan of action: _____
_____
_____

Prescribed medications: _____
_____

Follow up required: _____
_____
_____
_____
_____

Weight: _____ Blood Pressure: _____ Heart Rate: _____ Temp: _____

Prescribed Diagnostic Tests

Date: _____ Test ordered by: _____

Name of laboratory / hospital / facility: _____

Name of attending physician / laboratory rep: _____

Name of diagnostic test: _____

_____

Reason for test: _____

_____

Prep for test: _____

_____

Results of test: _____

_____

_____

_____

Date: _____ Test ordered by: _____

Name of laboratory / hospital / facility: _____

Name of attending physician / laboratory rep: _____

Name of diagnostic test: _____

_____

Reason for test: _____

_____

Prep for test: _____

_____

Results of test: _____

_____

_____

_____

Date: _____

Doctor's name: _____

Facility name / Phone: _____

Reason for visit: _____
_____

Symptoms: _____
_____
_____
_____

Questions: _____
_____
_____

Doctor's advice/Procedure performed: _____
_____
_____
_____
_____

Plan of action: _____
_____
_____

Prescribed medications: _____
_____

Follow up required: _____
_____
_____
_____
_____

Weight: _____ Blood Pressure: _____ Heart Rate: _____ Temp: _____

Prescribed Diagnostic Tests

Date: _____ Test ordered by: _____

Name of laboratory / hospital / facility: _____

Name of attending physician / laboratory rep: _____

Name of diagnostic test: _____

_____

Reason for test: _____

_____

Prep for test: _____

_____

Results of test: _____

_____

_____

_____

Date: _____ Test ordered by: _____

Name of laboratory / hospital / facility: _____

Name of attending physician / laboratory rep: _____

Name of diagnostic test: _____

_____

Reason for test: _____

_____

Prep for test: _____

_____

Results of test: _____

_____

_____

_____

Date: _____

Doctor's name: _____

Facility name / Phone: _____

Reason for visit: _____

Symptoms: _____

_____

_____

_____

Questions: _____

_____

_____

Doctor's advice/Procedure performed: _____

_____

_____

_____

_____

Plan of action: _____

_____

_____

Prescribed medications: _____

_____

Follow up required: _____

_____

_____

_____

_____

_____

Weight: _____ Blood Pressure: _____ Heart Rate: _____ Temp: _____

Prescribed Diagnostic Tests

Date: _____ Test ordered by: _____

Name of laboratory / hospital / facility: _____

Name of attending physician / laboratory rep: _____

Name of diagnostic test: _____

_____

Reason for test: _____

_____

Prep for test: _____

_____

Results of test: _____

_____

_____

_____

_____

Date: _____ Test ordered by: _____

Name of laboratory / hospital / facility: _____

Name of attending physician / laboratory rep: _____

Name of diagnostic test: _____

_____

Reason for test: _____

_____

Prep for test: _____

_____

Results of test: _____

_____

_____

_____

Date: _____

Doctor's name: _____

Facility name / Phone: _____

Reason for visit: _____

_____

Symptoms: _____

_____

_____

_____

Questions: _____

_____

_____

Doctor's advice/Procedure performed: _____

_____

_____

_____

_____

_____

Plan of action: _____

_____

_____

Prescribed medications: _____

_____

Follow up required: _____

_____

_____

_____

_____

_____

Weight: _____ Blood Pressure: _____ Heart Rate: _____ Temp: _____

Prescribed Diagnostic Tests

Date: _____ Test ordered by: _____

Name of laboratory / hospital / facility: _____

Name of attending physician / laboratory rep: _____

Name of diagnostic test: _____

_____

Reason for test: _____

_____

Prep for test: _____

_____

Results of test: _____

_____

_____

_____

_____

Date: _____ Test ordered by: _____

Name of laboratory / hospital / facility: _____

Name of attending physician / laboratory rep: _____

Name of diagnostic test: _____

_____

Reason for test: _____

_____

Prep for test: _____

_____

Results of test: _____

_____

_____

_____

Date: _____

Doctor's name: _____

Facility name / Phone: _____

Reason for visit: _____
_____

Symptoms: _____
_____
_____
_____

Questions: _____
_____
_____

Doctor's advice/Procedure performed: _____
_____
_____
_____
_____
_____

Plan of action: _____
_____
_____

Prescribed medications: _____
_____

Follow up required: _____
_____
_____
_____
_____
_____

Weight: _____ Blood Pressure: _____ Heart Rate: _____ Temp: _____

Prescribed Diagnostic Tests

Date: _____ Test ordered by: _____

Name of laboratory / hospital / facility: _____

Name of attending physician / laboratory rep: _____

Name of diagnostic test: _____

_____

Reason for test: _____

_____

Prep for test: _____

_____

Results of test: _____

_____

_____

_____

_____

Date: _____ Test ordered by: _____

Name of laboratory / hospital / facility: _____

Name of attending physician / laboratory rep: _____

Name of diagnostic test: _____

_____

Reason for test: _____

_____

Prep for test: _____

_____

Results of test: _____

_____

_____

_____

_____

Date: _____

Doctor's name: _____

Facility name / Phone: _____

Reason for visit: _____
_____

Symptoms: _____
_____
_____
_____

Questions: _____
_____
_____

Doctor's advice/Procedure performed: ____
_____
_____
_____
_____

Plan of action: _____
_____
_____

Prescribed medications: _____
_____

Follow up required: _____
_____
_____
_____
_____
_____

Weight: _____ Blood Pressure: _____ Heart Rate: _____ Temp: _____

Prescribed Diagnostic Tests

Date: _____ Test ordered by: _____

Name of laboratory / hospital / facility: _____

Name of attending physician / laboratory rep: _____

Name of diagnostic test: _____

_____

Reason for test: _____

_____

Prep for test: _____

_____

Results of test: _____

_____

_____

_____

Date: _____ Test ordered by: _____

Name of laboratory / hospital / facility: _____

Name of attending physician / laboratory rep: _____

Name of diagnostic test: _____

_____

Reason for test: _____

_____

Prep for test: _____

_____

Results of test: _____

_____

_____

_____

Every journal tells a story.

Barbara Morina, President and founder of Journals Unlimited, Inc. presents The "Write It Down!"® Series. With over 60 titles in print and several more in the works, The "Write It Down!" ® Series has become one of the most popular selling brands of personal journals.

I've always kept a personal journal to express my thoughts, excitement, and concerns for the moment and it helps me to plan and set goals for the future. Everyone experiences important events worth remembering. Whatever your age or passion, keeping a journal is a great way to capture and recall your thoughts and ideas, while recording all your precious memories.

With just an idea, the company was started in the summer of 1997. I was on vacation on the west coast of Michigan when I walked into a Barnes & Noble Book store. I wanted to pick up a Vacation journal and envisioned finding a series of journals with the prompts such as our journals offer (Where I travelled, Where I stayed, People I met, etc.). There was nothing even close, only a wide variety of blank journals. Almost immediately the idea was born!

I started with just four journal titles and began selling them at craft shows and personally calling on gift stores throughout Michigan. I now have over 100 salespeople representing a continually expanding line. It has been an empowering ride. The "Write It Down!" ® Series can be found in retail stores across the U.S.A. and Canada. In addition to the retail market we also print custom journals for specific client needs.

I have been truly blessed with the skill and professionalism of my staff. I was fortunate enough to discover at an early age that the key to success is to surround yourself with people who are smarter and more experienced than you.

The first page of all of my journals reads:
"Life is an adventure. It is not the destination we reach that's most rewarding. It's the journey along the way. So Write it Down! and treasure the memory forever... I guess that sums it up!"

Barbara Morina

President and Founder
Journals Unlimited, Inc.